Perennial

Books by Vivian Shipley

Poems out of Harlan County (1989)
Devil's Lane (1996)
Crazy Quilt (1999)
Fair Haven (2000)
When There Is No Shore (2002)
Gleanings: Old Poems, New Poems (2003)
Hardboot: Poems New & Old (2005)
All of Your Messages Have Been Erased (2010)

Chapbooks

Jack Tales (1982)
How Many Stones? (1998)
Echo & Anger, Still (1999)
Down of Hawk (2001)
Fishing Poems (2001)
Greatest Hits: 1974-2010 (2011)

Perennial

VIVIAN SHIPLEY

Negative Capability PRESS

MOBILE, ALABAMA

ISBN 978-0-942544-29-9
Library of Congress Control Number: 2015909400

Cover and interior design by Megan Cary
Author photograph by Wayne Chapman

Negative Capability Press
62 Ridgelawn Drive East
Mobile, Alabama 36608

www.negativecapabilitypress.org
facebook.com/negativecapabilitypress

For my husband

Edward Charles Harris

whose love is perennial

About the Cover

The photograph is of Celia Farmer who was Vivian Shipley's great-great-grandmother and lived to 107 on one small farm or another in Pulaski County, Kentucky. She was born July 4, 1818 and died June 20, 1925. The daughter of Peter and Jane Baker, she married James Farmer in May, 1839. Blind for many years, she had no teeth and was cared for at the end of her life by her daughter, Lydia Farmer Stewart who is Shipley's great-grandmother and the mother of her maternal grandmother, Parealy Bell Stewart. Parealy married Howard Todd. Their daughter, Alice Lee Todd, who was Shipley's mother, married Charles Vernon Shipley on December 23, 1939. Her parents are buried in the Howe Valley Methodist Church cemetery near the Shipley farm in Hardin County, Kentucky.

CONTENTS

I

II

III

I

DIGGING UP PEONIES

Overcoming fear of stalks that were too close,
I reminded myself it was Lexington, that mist

on fields meant rattlesnakes in rows of corn
would be cold, sluggish. Like prying out

potatoes with my fingers, I dug up tubers
as if I could lift my father, seeded with cancer,

if only for a day from gravity, from ground.
My parents knew what I knew—this was the end.

They wouldn't return to this house my father built.
No Ukrainian, wheelbarrowing my parents from

Russian missile attacks in Mariupol, I brought as
much of Kentucky, of their dirt as I could carry

on our flight to Connecticut. A bride, moving
to New Haven over forty years ago, I still had

not taken root. I cannot explain the urge I had
to go to creekstone fences my father stacked,

dig up box after box of peonies I banked into
Stony Creek granite piled along my side garden.

His last spring, propped up in the oak bed
his parents slept in on their wedding night

in Howe Valley, my father saw pink, white,
fuchsia, blossoming. Is this what revision is,

change of location, spreading, to retell my story
another time, in another soil? Unable to untie

what binds me to Kentucky, to bones of all
those who are in my bones, I saved what I

could of my mother, my father from this earth,
from the dissolution that binds us after all.

DON'T BUY
THE NEW HAVEN REGISTER

Catch the week on Saturday, again Sunday
when you scrub paint from white grey-veined
Vermont marble of Yale's Beinecke Library,
bronze and glass walls, shield for William Blake's
Songs of Innocence and of Experience with his *tyger*

and *lamb* you'll never get an afternoon off to see.
It's a sure bet a mayor won't erect a bronze statue
by Seward Johnson of you on the green: a man
thickened by age squatting in a Red Sox cap.
Mixing full strength ammonia with Top Job, you

scour the massacre of the week: 130 schoolchildren
in Pakistan by ISIS. Rectangular panels that filter
light are a perfect canvas for Connecticut's self
appointed night priests who layer graffiti with
aerosol cans. They've been your answer to prayers

for a steady job for fourteen years. At first, it was
Osama bin Laden, jihad, genocide in Sudan. Then,
swirls of green and yellow for Cairo's Arab Spring.
Lately, it's been S you erase: Syria, Sunni, Shiite,
Serbs. Eyes closed, you could remove Israel, Hamas,

Hezbollah spiraled in red, blue and black. Your boss
is generous, gives you fifteen minutes after punching
the clock, time to sit with coffee and a cigarette next
to Alexander Calder's sculpture, *Gallows and Lollipops*.
Death tolls never stop, this week Houthis in Yemen,

last week, Nigeria and Afghanistan. An inspiration
for over two weeks was Al-Qaeda's terrorist attack

on Parisian journalists. There wasn't much point in
removing *Je suis Charlie*. But, hey, paid by the hour
to clean, keep Hewitt Quadrangle, Beinecke's granite

geometry spotless, why should you care? Bless all
politicians who fuel protests, terrorists who inflame
them. Pray Yalies keep stenciling the library's white slabs.
Using Brillo pads on paint sprayed on concrete sidewalks
would be harder on your hands, your arms, your knees.

EVEN A GOOD CURSE
SHOULD NOT LAST FOREVER

Sadie might have said to her neighbor, *If your hog roots up my parsnips again, I hope she falls on the ground and dies.* The sow might have had a heart attack, might have been old when she keeled over like sails do in a storm. In Salem, Massachusetts, that would have been cause enough to call Sadie a witch, or to hang Rebecca Nurse on July 19, 1692.

To mark the anniversary, the three hundred years, Rebecca is re-visiting Salem in a Campaign Tours' bus decorated with brooms. Getting right into the spirit, the young, eager orthopedist seated by her at the Hawthorne Inn jokes with the waiter, wants to see witches' bones. Rebecca smiles; he won't find hers. Smuggled back to Pine Street by Francis, her husband, her body was entwined in roots of a tree where none would ever dig. There's a monument now, verses by Whittier. Let all these tourists read them — that's real revenge. Coming down the stairs of her old house, she can see the table and chairs have been replaced. No carpet on the floor, this is no longer the home she came to as a bride. In the garden, her children have not gathered in welcome. Hate still beats in her, hanging like a weight at the end of a pendulum or stones used to press Giles Corey to death. At first, Reverend Parris's daughter Betty and his niece Abigail wouldn't answer but screamed, writhed, dashed a Bible against the wall. Other children began to copy them, growled like bears, threw themselves on the floor in a fit. One tried to crawl into the fireplace. Fear of the Devil began to spread. Rebecca has forgiven Tituba, the Parris's slave, for confessing but remembers every word of testimony that branded her witch given by Sarah Holten, after her triumph of getting two black dogs hung in April for giving the evil eye.

Passing store mannequins outfitted as witches and Fatima's Parlor of Astrology with tarot cards, the guide reveals that Halloween is when the real fun begins. First stop: the Witch Dungeon Museum. Professional actresses reenact scenes in the dungeon that has been featured on *Good Morning America*. Next, Rebecca sits through a powerful half-hour multisensory presentation with 13 life-sized stage settings at the Salem Witch Museum. At the Old Town Hall, she is allowed to participate and reenact the witchcraft trial of Bridget Bishop, the first woman sentenced to hang by Judge Dross. It's AAA approved, unlike the Salem Wax Museum of Witches and Seafarers which does have a Gravestone Rubbing Station, and Dungeon and Trial scene. If her neck hadn't snapped when she was hung, Rebecca might have enjoyed *Three hundred years of spine-tingling history*. At the Salem Witch Village, Rebecca journeys back in time to discover myths and facts of witchcraft. Invited to confront grim realities of medieval hysteria, superstition and torture, learn truths behind the legends, each member of the group is asked to define what they think being a witch really meant. Untying the scarf from her neck, Rebecca pulls back her hair. Raw suffering burns with its own light, holds back nothing. The rope's curse ringing her neck curves like harbor lights of Marseilles or Istanbul.

Fortitude, a virtue, Rebecca refused to blame fear of altitude, to confess. Shining like revelation, the tree leaned to her. Rough, bark opened when she risked the leap as if trusting herself to water instead of rope. Just past daybreak, her body lifted over trees, dissolving timberline, breaking membrane of sky. Salem burned. Gleaming with last juice, her lips could not shape love. Her blood was already replacing itself. Landlocked, her husband, her children were faces she could not recognize. The sky was awash with her going; for another week, indigo refused to cloud. Three hundred years have not dissolved Rebecca's search for that last moment when she listened to her own breathing, before she lost the ground she stood on, before she was eased down. No longer thinking of corrections that might be made, testimony that could be given, notes fill her like a carillon of grace. What Rebecca has become bears no resemblance to what she was, as in chrysalis to moth.

History of Art: Instinct

Soul clap its hands and sing, and louder sing
　　—William Butler Yeats

I try to teach my son a song to hum
about love, its grace. Should I tell him how
Basil, Emperor of Byzantium,
took fourteen thousand captives, made them bow
as they were blinded? One in a hundred
kept an eye to guide the others, stumbling
home like six men strung by sticks, head to head,
in Pieter Bruegel The Elder's painting,
The Blind Leading the Blind. I choose to cull
Janson's pages that age Eric too soon.
Outside our cat has captured a young gull
caught in sea grass. Thinking I hear a loon,
we run, find the cry. I walk him to sand
against the day he takes this book in hand.

9

PERENNIAL

The crow doth sing as sweetly as the lark
When neither is attended.
        —William Shakespeare

Guilford, Connecticut Resident, Former Nazi Guard.
Below *The New Haven Register* headlines: it is you.
My next door neighbor for eighteen years, have you
been hovering over death camps, a helicopter, a drone,

or a dirigible, fearful someone would poke a hole
in your story, light a match? Accent of a distant place
clings like seeds of milkweed, but for the reporters,
your tongue, mute peninsula, drags up the sound for *no.*

Stooped at seventy-two, I calculate dead weight you
shouldered. My son's 4-H leader, you took nightly strolls
on the green with Dylan, your yellow lab. As October
shortened life, you remembered to feed sparrows

after the birdbath froze over. A newscaster calls me
for a live on-the-air interview. I should have suspected
something, knowing you raise pigeons to feed a falcon,
coops positioned like Siamese twins joined at the chest.

You never invited me to fields back of Bishop's Orchard
for a hunt. So, all day, I guillotine hosta, day lilies, hoping
you will come outside, tomatoes, zucchini in hand, to trade
your garden for mine. It's details that seduce me, to know

first hand in what position most died, get a metaphor
for bodies in box cars. A heart can talk itself into anything
while alibis revise themselves, but one story will finally
catch another off guard, crisscrossing. I stay alert, ready.

With arms elbowed on your fence, I rest, then start digging
again until dusk. I want to learn from you about power,
if it feels like being a pilot of a B-52 Stratofortress bomber
lumbering on a runway in England, tail lifting to make

Kosovo quake, evaporating those below into white noon sky?
To pass time, I play mental connect the dots with numbers you
rounded up, leveled to ash. Think, I might say, of Dachau,
of all who resisted you by staying alive, who wake as you do,

but with only the memory of mother, father, sister, brother,
you denied them. Pilgrims in a Holy Week procession,
some carry names, photos, some knowledge in their faces.
A conductor, your hand extended, have you emptied hair

from lockets, taken wedding rings, teeth? Neat, I imagine
you'd have toed out a cigarette burning in a dead man's hand.
You do not come out that first day, then the next, while
editorials debate what to do with you, murderer, torturer,

now that you have been found. To stave off impending
deportation what will you offer to do? Will you finally give
a widow notebooks from her husband's breastpocket,
poems she could read in sunlight to soothe her? Would

you say how ink, if not his breathwords, have been saved?
A week passes. I continue to mulch with the same need
that made me travel to see the Museo di Criminologia
Medioevale in San Gimignano, Italy, with torture devices

from The Inquisition when a death sentence was not about
quietness and efficiency. Thumbscrews, branding irons,
skull crushers, tongue clamps, the pear, spiked speculum,
were tucked away in a Tuscan hillside. My breath fogged

the glass. More than six feet tall, an iron maiden towered
in the corner. Spotlights were on a spiked interior, bread
and juice to keep the victim alive and alert. Description
of water torture was less visually interesting, unlike

a spiked chair which was wooden with inch-high studs.
There were even multimedia extras: a voice bellowing,
a woman who admitted guilt, pleaded for mercy. I left her.
Exiting, a smiling ticket taker, his wave, his *Buon giorno*

eased reentry into land as peaceful as that seen from trains
on the last ride Jews took from Lublin to Majdanek,
Belzec, and Sobibor. Straight sand paths funneled them
into flat Polish woods of birch and pine, millions of trees

like the dead, anonymous as their gravestones Germans
used to pave new road. As my neighbor, you have grown
safe, escaping into your daughters, their children. You lined
gardens with day lilies I clumped, bordered them in hosta

I shared. Each autumn, wind splayed our maple leaves
like shoes, hair carved into piles by guards as if dividing
beef: shank, loin, flank, round. I want to know what
you remember, shoveling clay from rock, sprinkling

bone meal like holy water on snowdrops, digging roses
to repot. What does the color of their pale roots trigger?
Your porch drips with wisteria, the lavender petals
like moth wings. Honeyed afternoons cannot lull me

into believing the years have erased the particulars I
want to hear. Darkness pulls the street lamp, bats dive
into halos alive with insects that don't know to fear light,
who are drawn to it as I am to you. A carrion crow

tugging at suet, your darkness is in me, lifts my wings
on air tasting of salt blown in from Long Island Sound.

CHRISTINE, AT NIGHT, I TIRED;
EARLY MORNING, I ...

Late January, the words I spoke outside my classroom
created no clear picture like workshop poems threaded
by your mother's suicide. To compare their techniques,
I assigned Plath and Sexton. Not satisfied, you asked
why Virginia Woolf weighted her pockets with stones,

concluding it was impossible to say just which one caused
her to sink. You quit coming to Southern, I didn't call; dead
all these months, I didn't know. Your anguish before me
like chain and mace in a museum, I gathered your work
to publish a chapbook. Boasting how I'd address your death

with a word of life, I wrote a preface saying how shortsighted
it was to die so close to spring, that we could have had an early
bonfire and as we tasted it, the scent of hickory smoke, though
sharp, would still live on our tongues. No Liberty Bell cruise
circling Long Island Sound, I could keep no schedule, boxed

your manuscript, just as I had the scotch plaid coat I was going
to put in the Goodwill dumpster. Your poems were thrown
out by movers emptying my desk. Another vow I didn't honor,
my promise to keep your name alive was hollow, an apple cored
by your death, but never peeled into lines of print. January sky,

coral as the high collared dress you last wore, or flashes of hair,
china black, startle me like a voice of a person I didn't know
was in the room. Nobody experiences anything through words:
think Hiroshima; Kyushu's port city, Nagasaki. Atomic bomb,
nuclear shadow are the same to a mother as she nurses her son

even after reading articles about warring white blood cells.
A mind adjusts to that just as after a time your pupils contracted

inside the closet where you hung among jackets, above shoes.
Was a vacuum kicked aside like women flinging bras in Filene's
Basement, or were you trying to pray, a mantis with legs slowly

lifting? The scene shifts. Perhaps a girl's wrists hadn't healed over
razor scars, perhaps the driver of a truck had swerved in time,
perhaps I had called you aside after class. Night mushrooms
into a cloud. What do I know about it or your mind, Christine,
thick with layers you couldn't peel off like strips of burned skin.

A Birthday Party
on Old Orchard Road

It's Fourth of July. On this one day we celebrate
freedom, it's okay to talk with our mouths full.
Hot dogs and chili are the prelude to salutes,

cherry bombs, lady fingers, Chinese. A clear prey
for crows, a beetle larger than a cockroach, gleaming
green then blue, ventures onto red flagstone around

the pool—an error, though the bug's last. Civilization
means nothing, but to honor Washington, we debate:
let's get a Dixie Cup and blow him to bits; tie a bottle

rocket, send him aloft; gas him with a smoke bomb;
ignite him with a sparkler. Waltzing around, we lift
our arms to vote; we are a democracy. Attracted by

spiders killing ants, Darwin wrote, *Efforts which the poor
little creatures made to extricate themselves from such a death
were wonderful.* No such sport, our beetle ignores strings

of fireworks, circling like a necklace of coral laid flat.
Five, four, three, two, one, Boom! Does shock ripple
his shell, bones rattling as beans in a maraca do? Need

for sound, smoke satisfied, we reel off statistics: drugs,
violence, a New Haven father who burned two initials
on his son's forearm with cigarettes. We wonder why.

YET WE WERE WRONG, TERRIBLY WRONG.

—Robert S. McNamara, Secretary of Defense, 1961-1968

Dressed in a black three-piece suit with a roll of toilet paper
    in one hand and a Bible in the other, your brother starts
at the corner of Wooster Square Park on Chapel Street
    then parades until he spots an elm that suits him. Before

spending two years in Vietnam, he would walk up State Street
    to the front window of the drug store and stand
by Joseph Rosenthal's AP photograph of an American flag
    being raised on Mt. Suribachi at the top of Iwo Jima.

In WWII, when the Fifth Marine Division made it to the summit
    after four days of battle, your father was one of six men
who raised the flag. He died within days. It was late February,
    early March of 1945. There were banners in the windows

with stars on them. Blue meant someone from that house
    was in the service and a gold star meant someone had died.
Your grandmother's house had three stars, two blue, one gold.
    Then another turned to gold. Your brother still has the letters

written by your father about the firefights: Marines would hold
    weapons over a ridge, exposing only hands and upper arms
to return fire. Letters were filled with Ira Hayes, a Pima Indian
    who also raised the flag but who survived to die of alcohol.

Hayes would pop up to shoot, flop back down to reload. During
    one mortar attack, he walked off to relieve himself.
Six thousand, two hundred died on Iwo Jima in shallow gulches,
    from snipers, shells being lobbed. Hayes was the soldier

your brother wanted to be when he enlisted and asked to be
    shipped to Da Nang. There were no flags to raise, no pictures
in *The New Haven Register*, no stars in windows. Not a battle
    statistic like your father, your brother is unable to drown

himself in shots and beers like Hayes. He will take nothing
        from the living, but cannot stop what the dead drain
out of him. Shouting at the elm tree about bodies splitting
        apart, your brother hurls the roll of paper high into air.

Is each layer a beginning, wiping out years in Vietnam that are
        like ice on the window spreading into a jungle of ferns
or waiting fingers? Streaming like a rocket unrolling all the way
        to heaven, the tissue always misses the branches and piles

in the street. Shrugging it off, your brother goes back home
        to your mother who never complains about the mess,
but worries over the extravagance of it, the waste of good paper.
        Your cousin Joyce stuffed cotton in her cheeks to fill them

out, but she didn't throw it away. Dried overnight, the balls were
        used again and again. The toilet paper is useless, melting
into the street like years your brother spent waiting in the dark,
        knowing every stumbling place his hand might touch down

on a face. Eyes were always open, darker than veined cocoa
        leaves or concentrated like pools of light in silk from Hanoi.
Sucked back, your brother confronts the eyes and your father,
        the look on his face, as he braces to raise the flag, making

shoulders ache with the permanence of it. No Joseph Rosenthal
        photograph of your brother in the drug store, no red, white,
and blue only a black marble wall of eyes that will never close,
        that will never disappear, that words of remorse cannot erase.

CHARLIE'S AT THE WIRE
WAITING FOR YOU TO SLEEP

—for B.R.

Your weekly poems were reruns: prisoners of pirates walking
the plank. In San Francisco, you jumped, hiding long black dreads
under a red bandana to imitate your father who tied one around

his head, dipped in blood from bodies that could not deny him.
At ten, lighting up Camels without filters, you knew hands didn't
leave the same marks as a belt. Dope sick at Thanksgiving, you

ranted about nine months of signing in on a yellow visitor pad
printed in black: *National Center for Post Traumatic Stress Disorder.*
Your hands in jeans to stop the shaking, a night watch belched

you down white tile threading a beige corridor. Your father sat
on paper sheets that ripped with weight, holding a Dixie cup
of orange juice for his pills. Once big as pythons, his arms were

stems, leafed in scars latticed over crosses, death unit insignias.
Fingering a necklace of withered ears beaded by kidney stones,
he would start with sweat on skin, then the helicopter droning

like the West Haven VA ventilation system, the elephant grass.
Predictable, your father ended with the tiger cage, boasting about
earning his blood bandana again, again. A half-gallon of Dewars

every two days did not drown drums from your father's funeral
that you kept sounding out on a xylophone of bones he brought
to your mother from razor mountains in Pleiku, South Vietnam.

Bill, last April, sitting on rocks at Morgan Point, my words lifted
you. Caught in a down draft, you were drawn back, compared
birds to chalk, undissolved by the wave's tongue, to the pill

you found too bitter to chew: your father stalking, spearing
shadows, leaving holes for eyes. Unerring as gulls plunging to
beak mussels they had dropped, going back to New Haven

in the back seat of my car, I knew you'd shoot up, probing
until you found a vein that would open, to feel that rush you
needed to keep Charlie at the wire, to keep you from sleep.

AND WE ARE HERE
AS ON A DARKLING PLAIN

It's June, afternoon, Matthew Arnold's line
from *Dover Beach* can't obliterate ripe
brie or casaba melon on the tine
of my fork. Red pistachios I wipe
off of my fingers rival the full glass
of burgundy for color splashed on back
drop of Long Island Sound. Waves start to mass
off rocks of Morgan Point. There is no lack
of water, brown sand to streak. Will there be
an end? Such bleak perspective undoes life.
I close the book on white cliffs, on the sea
and the *grating roar of pebbles*. All strife
is blocked when my son, Matthew, of six full
months puts his mouth onto my breast to pull.

WERE GUARDS IN PERM 36 READING SHAKESPEARE?

But I will find him when he lies asleep,
And in his ear I'll holla 'Mortimer!'
Nay,
I'll have a starling shall be taught to speak
Nothing but 'Mortimer,' and give it him
To keep his anger still in motion.
        —*Henry IV, Part I*

Vasyl Stus, outside your cell in Kachino, Russia, did men
fear your poems more than bricks, more than bullets?
They may have learned power in a word from Hotspur

as he trained a starling to gall and pinch Bolingbroke.
Ukrainian, you earned the Russian title for inmate, *zek*—
a badge I can't pin on while touring Perm 36, a stop

on a summer boat tour of the Gulag and a fifty mile
bus ride from Lysva. I see why Stalin never allowed
photographs or films of Soviet labor camps. Vasyl Stus,

a guide will not allow me to sandpaper my hand
on cement walls of a punishment cube where you died.
No cause, just September 4, 1985. No death camp

like Kolyma or Magadan, you could not have expected to
be murdered one month before the Nobel Prize you were
nominated for was announced. Buoyed by hope poems

would speak for you in Stockholm, you didn't live to hear
Claude Simon named. Your body was tied to earth, hooked
as if on a rod held in hands slowly reeling you in to a death

that must have been your salvation. Blackened with mildew,
with rot, wooden shacks cluster at Perm 36. Green on green,
painted guard towers are the only sign of life in this camp.

Natan Sharansky, Sergei Kovalyov, Vladimir Bukovsky
and Sevko Lukyanenko. All ghosts, all vanished
like you, Vasyl Stus. Hanging over rails of the tour boat,

I saw no sign of the twenty million other bodies
bulldozed or smothered by snow drifts in the chain
of prisons and labor camps that link the Gulag, wind

Ural Mountains like lights on an evergreen. Walking
into a maximum security room, a tourist, I can't imagine
being starved, flayed, my eyes being toed like glowing

coals by a boot and my legs, a forest fire being stamped
out. Unrecorded, a voice without throat to channel it
disappears, memory of a name thickens to amnesia,

then vanishes if there are no words to print it, no starling
Hotspur coached to speak it. Each morning, four to six men
from each cell crossed this narrow corridor where I stand

to finger workroom bars as if feeling for a weak spot.
Vasyl Stus, when you were a free man, you walked about,
opened, closed books, sat down in a chair, then another,

fingers hooking a pen. Here in Perm 36, your hands hung,
meaty growths from your shoulders. With no thought
to scissor it, each day was like the next, pointless. Rubbing

thin striped-cotton uniforms you wore even when cold
pared down to your bone, I sit down on an iron bunk bed
you might have coiled on, kneel at the hole that served

as both sink and toilet. In the exercise yard, six by six feet,
my neck cranes, I try to spear sky slivering the crosshatched
barbed wire. Vasyl Stus, did a nail splintering wood remind

you of points of light around a star, of what you would not
see again, moon washing a field to bronze, show of deer,
light from a bar over the street? I see the ceiling you saw

before you fainted. What can I know of what is done
behind cement blocks to break a man's spirit, what is
done to break a man's body? What can I know of what

was done to you, how your breath was taken in this room
I visit? A starling or construction worker's wolf whistle,
I will call, arousing every ear that sleeps. Vasyl Stus,

Vasyl Stus, Vasyl Stus, echo and anger, still.

SPIDERS

If you dare, sit quietly in a Syrian market
or better yet and safer, a field, and it will
hum. Droning above goldenrod, there are
honeybees, yellow jackets and bumblebees.
Some are bee-mimics, harmless flies
that look and sound like stinging insects.
Some are not. All are looking for nectar,
some for blood. Hidden in forsythia are
yellow spikers, jumping spiders that never
bother with webs, instead like Islamist
women Chechen suicide bombers,
nicknamed *shahidka,* black widow spiders,
they ambush their prey, leaping with
deadly accuracy. Orb spiders web, hang
glistening in late-summer sun, droop
under weight of early dew. Straddling
center, or crouched at edge, holding
guy wires, each waits for the tremble.

BIRDSONG FOR SEPTEMBER 11, 2001

A robin is nesting at eye level in a blue spruce just outside
my bedroom. Preoccupied during the day with its safety,

each morning, again before dark, I check on her. I'm quiet;
she's still. Movement is what attracts my cat when making

a kill. Declawing Tatiana is out; three cats live next door.
The robin's eyes are black beads of Emily Dickinson's bird,

frightened as those of a boy held by his mother in the middle
of charred Nagasaki. Photographed by Alfred Eisenstaedt

four months after the atomic bomb, they sit on what was
a tree. Everything else is dead. The boy tucks his right hand

into his sweater vest armhole; the mother has a string of hair
blowing across her nose, her mouth a crescent moon, perfect

in its downward curve. What would she make of my obsession
with a bird's life? Crawling out from under death, would

she resonate Arviragus's cry in *Cymbeline?* Holding Imogen,
believing his sister to be dead, he laments: *I'll sweeten thy sad*

grave. . . the ruddock would, With charitable bill. Many centuries
old, robins are Anglo Saxon ruddocks, have power over

the dead's repose. Will my unborn birds requiem this mother,
her son, Japanese children a camera did not catch and hold,

ones ensnared by the twentieth century, its hundred years
of genocide? It could be April, 1915; I could be in Havav

as Turks dispose of one and a half million Armenians.
If the robin does not get to hatch these eggs that worry me,

no notes will trill each September 11th for 2,823 lives lost
when terrorists tried to outdo the last century's statistics:

Stalin's purging; the Holocaust vaporizing millions of Jews;
China's Cultural Revolution; Iraq gassing Kurds; Rwanda;

Serbs' cleansing of Muslims. Too many millions to recall,
too much death for a single song or bird, but each life that

went unrecorded on paper or film held breath, had nested
as two blue eggs of my robin do. Will these fledglings bear

witness to two planes in 2001 exploding, one, then another?
The first twin tower, a deck of cards dropping, the second

joining the avalanche—all live, a television broadcast of men,
women, who chose air rather than fire, dropping to pavement.

I'll keep watch so robins hatch to symphony these dead, keep
memory for the twenty-first century. Tatiana, my calico, kills

from instinct, has claws, but she's not calculating like suicide
bombers strapped in fuel-filled jets, timing impact for numbers.

There is no metaphor. Birdsong can not float so much death
or dirge the cries still swelling, bursting, to mourn this day

of death, September 11, 2001. The Nagasaki mother holds
her future, hands cupping joy of her son's life. Children of 343

firefighters will never be held by arms that lifted others to life.
My robins haven't hatched; this century is not two decades old.

I'll crate my cat, do what I can to preserve life, however small.

No Deliverance

—September 11, 2006

Long, unbroken, heat has driven a raccoon
to mouth water in trays holding philodendron
I have positioned to catch early morning sun.
With no words to share, no sign language,
to communicate, maybe to show my power
over physical need this animal cannot control,
I set out a slaking bowl. All I do is crater
withered grass with white ceramic. Untouched,
the water stands all day as if it held my scent.
Remembering smoke, towers, planes, bodies
in air I'd witnessed mid-morning five years
ago, I twist my hair around a finger as I watch
the feral eyes rimmed in black that punctuate
arborvitae binding my yard. If I could unzipper
the scar from a brain tumor that connects scalp
hooding my skull and pull skin down to unmask
vessels, a tame heart beating, I might cut razor
wire fear that keeps this raccoon away, stops it
from assuaging the thirst for life we both share.

ODE TO VIRGINIA TECH, BLACKSBURG: APRIL 16, 2007

Mockingbirds don't do one thing but make music
—Harper Lee

The Monday after Thanksgiving was a school holiday
that unleashed us to hunt with our fathers for the first day

of deer season and soak plaid shirts with entrails of a buck.
In Lejunior, Kentucky, after mopping off coal dust, we ate

at kitchen tables stained with blood from squirrel meat
chopped up for burgoo. Disney's *Swamp Fox*, each January

I killed a squirrel for the tail to sew onto my cap. Hell bent
on fun, cruelty was as irrelevant as lightning bugs I smeared

to make fences phosphorescent. Summer, copperheads came
from woods to sun on black top. Mothers came running.

One pitch-forked the body while another hoed off the head.
As if pardoning sinners, our neighbor bagged long ones

in burlap in case the spirit moved her husband to take up
serpents at Pentecostal Church of God. Going to the dump

at dusk with an air rifle, I never blew away rats but if a pellet
hit an empty can, a possum would jump, metal armoring

its nose. My aim was better with a Wrist Rocket. Ball bearings
or a stone worked best. Coke from roadside gravel was light

as cork, too porous to hurt anything. Take aim, then pull back
surgical tubing and the leather pouch became a catapult. Never

stopping to think what I did could not be undone, I targeted
the red breast of a robin which had lured me with its music.

Remembering the silence, bird wings spread into a cross
on the ground, why do I wonder how Seung-Hui Cho

could harm the blameless, those he didn't know, pull a trigger
again, again until he had silenced thirty-two lives in mid-song?

Fifteen Minutes

You are Aziz Cici, a gypsy. You fire a shot in the dark.
    Not uncommon in Ukraine, but your bullet strikes
and kills Fatos Gremi, a *gadjo*. He is a rival thief, a drunk

and he has been throwing rocks at your window all night.
    One neighbor says seven, another midnight, a third
the hour before dawn. A pantomime at first, you don't mean

to kill him; you don't want a corpse to drag into the house.
    You don't like folding him into a burlap sack, asking
your wife Jeta to help you lug him to your car. Driving

to a local bridge, squeezing rocks in between legs and arms
    to fill the space, you roll him into Kalmius River. By dawn,
the water is low, and Fatos Gremi is an outcrop on the shore.

You're an outlaw. You tried to hide in Donetsk; tomorrow you
    will go on trial. Your white three room house perched over
a railroad track is empty, except for cousins who sit toe to toe

in opposite chairs. Competing for roles in your play, they're
    having fun creating the drama anew. A chicken appears
in the narrow strip between their feet. They start to talk about

the chicken: where had it come from, who owned it, should
    they stick it in a pot before a *gadjo* claims it? The biggest
question now is if red spots on its beak are chicken plague.

THE FAITHFUL COLT

—William Michael Harnett, 1890

Left hand caressing his pistol, Wadsworth Atheneum's guard
has his arms crossed, but I am still scared that the man by me
will reach for Harnett's painted revolver, snare drumming
bullets to jostle my heart. Dressed like he's from Kentucky,
I picture him in a Harlan County shotgun house up on cinder
blocks where a child with any sense knew it was not safe to
get up during the night for a drink of water. Looking twisted
as a tin roof hooked by wind, I doubt this man cares Harnett
had parental influence on Modrian's geometrical abstractions.

Does he know his eyes are being fooled, that *trompe l'oeil*
has objects occupy a shallow space so appearance of reality
is not spoiled by parallax shift if a viewer moves? Luminosity,
texture no photograph can provide, three dimensions in two,
cry out to be touched. Even birds flew down to peck chips
from purple grapes painted by the ancient Greek, Zeuxis.

As a shield, to impress this man I fear, should I spout how
Harnett's *The Old Violin* at Cincinnati's 1886 Industrial Expo
was so realistic that a woman tried to pull it from the wall
for her virtuoso son to play? Even Niccolo Paganini could
not finger music from *The Faithful Colt* slanted on a crazed
wooden panel, cracked white hunting horn handle up, double
barrel down, trigger hooked on a rusty nail that bleeds.

The museum brochure says William Harnett allows the eye
and mind to feel. That's why I watch hands of the man next
to me. It's noon. The guard, and then man move on. Alone,
I wonder what if Samuel Colt hadn't received a 1836 patent
for the revolving cylinder containing 5 or 6 bullets, innovative
cocking device. Would a gunman still have flint lock pistols,
single or double shot muskets, have to pause, break a barrel
open, insert one or two rounds and then close the gun to fire?

There would be no headlines:

April 20, 1999. Columbine High School, Littleton, Colorado.
13 dead, 21 wounded. Eric Harris fired a Hi-Point 995 Carbine
96 times, nicknamed his Savage Springfield 67 H shotgun,
Arlene *from* Doom. *Dylan Klebold in a black tee shirt*
stenciled with Wrath *in red shot a TEC-9 handgun 55 times.*

April 16, 2007. Virginia Tech, Blacksburg, Virginia.
32 dead, 17 wounded. Too many Glock 19 and Walther P 22
bullets to count. Seung-Hui Cho established the record
for the deadliest shooting by a single gunman in US history.

July 12, 2012. Century 16's showing of The Dark Knight,
Aurora, Colorado. 12 people killed, 58 wounded. James Holmes
dyed his hair orange. Smith & Wesson M&P 15 with a 100 round
drum magazine, back up Glock 22s, 12 gauge Remington 870.

What if Colt Manufacturing Company topped by gold stars
on a blue onion dome had not been founded across from
a river in Hartford, CT less than fifty miles from Newtown?.
Without a Bushmaster AR-15 assault rifle, could Adam Lanza
have massacred 20 children, 6 adults on December 14, 2012,
in Sandy Hook Elementary classrooms, first graders 6 and 7
years old sprawled, up to 12 bullets pumped into each?

If William Harnett's *The Faithful Colt* had stayed a canvas on
the Atheneum's gallery wall, would Newtown's cemetery
of twenty-six cardboard angels and twenty silken angels, white
as doves on Christmas trees, wing to life, pull off bedsheets
of mourning suffocating those with tombstones in their hearts?

Action News, Channel Eight

It's not the woman crying, her dead son,
unfenced tracks, or train and driver we rehash.

It is the camera, the photographer who kept
filming, zooming in for a close up of her face

while a policeman held the mother back right
as she learned who was dead. A passer-by took

pictures with his iPhone; staying outside yellow
tape, two girls posed, sticks in hand, for a selfie.

Clouds pack Morgan Point's sky; a blue heron
slips on pink granite rocks while spearing a fish,

and we laugh so hard, our back issues of *Poetry*
slide off the chaise. If our eyes closed, would

last night's six o'clock news, twisted lips, intrude?
In a day or so, if we pause, we probably won't think

of the mother's mouth, of her in the kitchen, no
son, no reason to fry morning bacon he can't smell.

Explosion of the Powder Magazine in Delft

—Daniel Vosmaer, 1654, Wadsworth Atheneum

Did Daniel Vosmaer know time between The Delft Thunderclap
and its aftermath was unbridgeable? His painting stops, stills me,
even though he makes no attempt to speak with his straw brown
oil strokes and dark grey smudges for thousands wounded, over
a hundred killed. Like Cornelis Soetens, Keeper of the Magazine,
opening a door October 12, 1654 to sample 40 tons of gunpowder,
nothing had prepared me for erasure. Swanning around, jazz band

vamping in me, I was sure luck was due to character, hard work.
No noise, smoke, vapor rising—the unthinkable—heard or felt
throughout Holland, Utrecht and the island of Texel for me.
There was suddenness, life avalanching when forty years ago
a brain tumor big as a baseball spelunked the right frontal lobe
of my brain. Curled like wild columbine in winter, it had rested
waiting for spring to knead me into seizures that would leave me

unable to ransom an entire year. Does Vosmaer's canvas unbolt me
because human form is almost absent? Minute figures in rubble,
intact roofs are inverted funnels, others could be ribbed triangular
bird cages. Like football goals, church spires of Oude and Nieuwe
Kerk frame the ruins. Free of debris, ground is punctuated by men
over a body; a boy runs to see like parents did in Bath, Michigan,
May 18, 1927. For a year, thinking the unthinkable, Andrew Kehoe

mapped out anger by lining sticks of dynamite under Bath's school,
hijacking 38 children, 7 to 14 years old, 6 adults and injuring 58.
Other things had gone wrong—a hornet's nest bursting, a horse
jumping a fence, but not this, not this. Paperwork of death, armada
of 100,000 cars driving by on Saturday to gawk or grieve, in three
days, Bath no longer headlined front pages because *Lucky Lindy*
flew from Long Island to Paris. Still, for weeks, hands with split

nails pawed brick and timber, ransacking the school for a child's
jacket sleeve, for understanding. Killing his wife, fire-bombing

his barn after he'd wired the horse's legs together, Andrew Kehoe stenciled a message for Bath Township on a wooden sign posted on his farm's fence: *Criminals are made, not born.* Daniel Vosmaer might have painted the school's roof after collapsing, but not children catapulting, feet, hands like playing cards thrown into air.

Sudden as The Delft Thunderclap or shifting of tectonic plates, Bath was the worst mass murder in a US school, but not as deadly as Texas on March 18, 1937. New London Consolidated School detonated minutes before classes were to be dismissed. Odorless, colorless natural gas leaking from heating units in an unventilated basement was ignited by a spark from a saw used in shop class. Rising off the foundation, the school hovered, then a cloud of ash,

debris plowed the earth. PTA mothers nearby in a gym were pulled to a confetti of paper which settled on bodies of over 300 children. A woman stood shaking her head like a dog emerging from a pond. Clasping ears to stop the echo, the screams, unable to scissor faces in photos, there was no way to unthread memory cross stitched in arms and legs. New London crutched through a silence of fifty years until a museum, no Atheneum, but a museum and a tea shop,

opened. Unlike barren trees with branches antlered toward heaven, Vosmaer positioned to the right of Delft's powder keg, a seedling would grow from New London's stump: malodorant, a thiol, was added in natural gas to signal, *leak*. In Connecticut, fifty miles from where I am, if an odor not silencers had been added to guns, could Adam Lanza have killed 20 Newtown, Connecticut first graders in Sandy Hook Elementary School? December 14, 2012, children

scattered like crazed pinballs, knocking over desks, easels, chairs. Each bullet in a child, in teachers, mother hens who shielded them, was like Delft Thunderclap, explosions in New London and Bath. Sudden, loud, final, a schism. It's a new year; ebony crows cinder fresh snow. Newtown can never be new again. It is New England but forty parents will never be rising sap in sugar maples. No need for hammered spiles. I know why there is nothing to tap. Forty

years ago with no *ikigai*, Okinawan for a reason to wake up, each
morning I thought of death, fingered an acrylic plate in my skull
where a brain tumor had been. The day came I unclenched teeth,
learned not only to speak but to sing—not for joy, no more notes
of jazz, but for release of sound leaving my body. No art expert,
I ask Atheneum's guide why Vosmaer while painting the powder
magazine at Delft positioned a man in a wide black brimmed hat

in front of a walkway arched like a tombstone leading to a ruin.
Shawled in a red cape, the man stands as if taunting a bull or death.
Was it for splash of color? Or, had Vosmaer learned as I did from
a wren building a nest in razor wire coiled on rooftops of Paterson,
New Jersey that nothing ever explodes hope in the living. Like
breath, despair cannot be held forever; like a monarch butterfly,
new life cannot be unfolded from its cocoon until it is its time.

KYRIE ELEISON

Battell Chapel's windows now dimming
from afternoon, you stand, no Beethoven
playing his last piano sonata *to peer at*
darkness through the bright eye of the world.
Plants in Yale's Old Campus are only swiss
chard, the rest withered shadows from *Job.*
You wish you could praise God as Bach did
sound rising, *Ja komm, Herr Jesu komm,*
but like fingernails on a chalkboard, sirens
in B flat interrupt this February gloom.
Where are New Haven's halcyon days?
You marked off seven days in a row
of bad weather. Inside, watching too much
morning, afternoon and evening news, you
can't keep from thinking: Guantanamo Bay,
waterboarding. Pacing does not block thought
of Nigeria, Boko Haram killing a woman
in labor just as the head of her son emerges
from her body. *Kyrie eleison, Kyrie eleison,*
Lord have mercy, Lord have mercy on
the born and unborn soul. Focus, not
on the Jordanian pilot ISIS burned alive
in a cage, but practice, *Jesu Christi,* your entry
as baritone for the quartet in Verdi's *Requiem.*
Throat muscles atrophy: *Jesu Christi.* You need
daffodils, not winter weeds disappearing to gray.

QUOTH THE RAVEN, 'NEVERMORE'

—Edgar Allan Poe

2015. Balloons must be set aloft by Pope Francis
as January ends with his gesture of peace; last year,
a pair of doves he released were swept down upon

by a crow, then a gull as if birds mimiced humans.
2012. Newtown, CT Sandy Hook Elementary.
Adam Lanza's trigger cannot be unpulled. Bullets

cannot be recalled to their AR-15 Bushmaster
barrel, six minute stream, 3 to 12 in 26 bodies.
A six year-old girl in a white tee-shirt glittering

with a peace sign like a bulls eye was an early
target. Terror like a riding crop banging Morse
code into chests of first graders, teachers crying,

flee little hummingbirds: pink cowboy boots; a boy
who loved to sing, spike his hair with gel;
another who will never get his two front teeth.

Can *Psalm 147* help the mother of a girl who
loved purple? He *heals the brokenhearted, and binds
up their wounds. He gives to the beasts their food*

and to the young ravens who cry. If Poe's raven
could beguile even one *sad soul into smiling,*
I'd begin a lecture by quoting Shakespeare's

Julius Caesar: when *Ravens, crows, and kites, fly
o'er,* if one flaps steadily, tail wedge-shaped,
it is a raven not a crow. Ravens do not caw,

they quork, knock, mumble, low, deep or ear
splitting then back to a whisper. Pointy feathers
on necks, curved bill partially covered with

feathers of bluish purple sheen, plumage is
black. Legs and feet are black—a bird of doom.
Shrouding bodies on battlefields, ravens did more

than foretell death, they directed predators to prey,
then waited to pick. There is better press in the Bible
when the Lord speaks to Elijah: *I have commanded*

the ravens to feed you.....And the ravens brought him bread
and meat in the morning, and bread and meat in the evening.
Twenty sets of parents have lost a child to feed,

any reason to rise in morning and have no appetite
for evening. In *Titus Andronicus*, Tamora speaks of
a *fatal raven*, but Lavinia replies, *some say that ravens foster*

forlorn children. No more quotes for me, but action;
I'll crate ravens for Newtown's children. Birds will do
half-barrel rolls while flying, slide down snow banks

on their backs. These ravens won't let death, mutilation
be a language taught in Sandy Hook Elementary classes,
but will put on a play, use twigs as tools, pull a string

to retrieve a treat. Like the raven in *Aesop's Fables,* they
will drop pebbles in a bowl to raise water until it reaches
beaks. Surely first graders will laugh as ravens drop bullet

size stones, then swoop to recall, catch them in mid-air.

Samaritan's Purse
Is in Monrovia, Liberia

I'm next in line at Dixwell Avenue Stop and Shop
reading *The New York Times'* front page article
about a woman with ebola who pleaded with
a Samaritan Purse's doctor for a cucumber
straight from the market. 2015. She's a survivor:
14 years of civil war, 200,000 killed. Shielded by
ritual sacrifice of her village's children, generals
stormed into battle wearing only shoes and a gun.
Toting teddy bear backpacks, 10 year-old soldiers
wielded M16s; rapists wore Halloween masks
and wedding gowns. Not today. The woman's
front page smile scythes the lumpy green skin,
the translucent flesh. The next day, she will die.

Artichokes, strawberries, asparagus, turkey
for economy, I figure up the total and count bills
to speed up my check out, but the woman in front
of me sorts out coins. I'm impatient, even though
I can see she's old with a hole in her sweater big
enough for me to stuff my fist through. Leave some
for bus fare, the checkout clerk urges. Light bulbs
are left behind. I'm the type who drops dollar bills
in Salvation Army buckets. Naturally, I buy the pack,
feel good as the bagger nods. I rush from the store
just as the woman has been helped up the steps
and boards the bus. I bring no light, bridge no gulf.

Reading William Hazlitt's
On the Pleasure of Hating

Red-shouldered, sharp-shinned, a red-tailed hawk
screams over my backyard. Rabbits flatten their ears,
squirrels press into branches. Songbirds freeze.

Adrenalin pumping, there is no breath. The keening
hawk chooses prey, drops like a sandbag, needle talons
first, or sails the horizon. Either way, songbirds cock heads,

squirrels rocket treetops. Their day is not interrupted
by death. They do not cower as I do listening to today's
news: April 2, 2015, Nairobi, Kenya, al-Shabab killed 142

Christian students in Garissa University dorm rooms.
Have I been novocained by statistics? Last week, March 25,
a Lufthansa pilot locked controls to descend and crash

into French Alps near Le Vernet. Piling higher and higher,
blanketed by weight of 150 lives coffined in Flight 9525,
I read Hazlitt's 1826 essay sitting in front of my gas logs.

Could it be *On the Pleasure of Hating* is true? *Animals
torment and worry one another without mercy: children kill flies
for sport: every one reads the accidents and offences in a newspaper.*

9/11/2001: unable to look away from the television,
from the World Trade Center, I watched as bodies were
catapulted, as some refused to be sacrificed to the volcano.

Flames gulping shirts, trousers, in pairs, holding hands,
couples made plans: a parachute of curtains or jackets.
A woman elbowed her laptop, her dear life, while she

stepped as if over a curb into air. I do not like to believe
William Hazlitt is describing me: *there is a secret affinity,
a hankering after, evil in the human mind.* Am I thrill-seeking

in airports when I look for abandoned purses or backpacks
to see where a bombing might happen? Impossible to
corral the internet videos of beheadings by black hooded

jihadis, there is also no way for me to deny, *The white
streak in our own fortunes is brightened or just rendered visible
by making all around it as dark as possible.* I wonder, would

Hazlitt ridicule me, call writing this poem an indulgence
because I can give thanks my three sons did not die on 9/11,
picture magnet the refrigerator with grandchildren, grateful

they weren't killed huddling in a classroom? Red tailed hawks
will return. There's no way to be a squirrel, rabbit, songbird
who are like bluebonnets in Texas—trampled, they spring

back. I'm not able to cremate memories of all these deaths;
my heart, mechanical as a metronome, still ticks off time,
refuses to be stilled by those I did not know, could not love.

II

LOVE—

vine Strangle Weed Dodder
words for a parasite you'll find
always wrapped around another
wild species are the ones to look for
on the ground
a seed germinates like any other
not particular but quick
the shoot suckers any type any place
once it's found a ventricle of another
the roots die
the love-vine needs no contact
with soil feeding
germinating right in the capsule

eliminates earth and time spent
to locate another
like Oedipus
some vines keep it in the family
flax Dodder grows only on flax
then strangles it
clover dodder feeds only on beans
then infects them
hard to detect no leaves
inconspicuous flowers
by the time you see
the intense orange of its stem
it's summer it's too late

Top Seven Sensations

—for T. I.

On the cover of *Richmond Magazine,* Julep's pheasant
crowns the food list. You insist I order it as your treat,
taking pleasure in what you can afford. Shockoe Slip
where *True Virginia Hospitality Still Exists* is a must-see,
but Oregon Hill where you were raised might as well
not exist. You were four, father gone, your mother
raised you and two brothers sleeping top to tail.
Never selling moonshine out windows, a waitress

who scrubbed floors, toilets, even ran a gas station,
I wonder if there's a woman like her in Julep's kitchen.
If she walked past us, would she be pleased to see
you here? Refusing to feed the tapeworm of memory,
your mother's the reason you never sit facing a window.
Oregon Hill was the only place she could pay weekly
rent. Shotgun house slanted on cinder blocks, you could
roll a marble front to back. No front step up to the door,

plumbing never installed, the roof's tin lid was bent
over like your mother. Wishing you Merry Christmas,
the landlord shoved your couch piled with clothes out
to the street; your plates too chipped to steal, brimmed
with rainwater until rent was paid. Even collard greens
your mother grew were choked by cocklebur, ragweed.
Cardboard in her shoes and aspirin melting in bad teeth,
she never walked streets like other women did as long

as their bodies held firm. Not allowed to hang around
at the corner of Pine and China Streets where more
murders occurred than any other place in Richmond,
you didn't meet Dugan Woods, the crime lord, who
held forth there, probably murdering a man or two
while he was at it, police being on his payroll and all.
Taking books from Richmond Public Library, proud to
know Tom Wolfe read his first books there, you waited

as if in a darkroom for a picture of yourself to emerge.
Enrolled in St. Andrew's Episcopal School for children
from Oregon Hill, your mind took shape. In a trinity
of reason: premise, condition, conclusion, instead you
sought cause. Going to the movies, you could not relax,
had to move from seat to seat if a man sat next to you,
knowing he wouldn't even bother to grope your knee.
No other way to scrub off dirt, the shower at the YMCA

was a gauntlet you had to run. The State Penitentiary
was next door to you in Oregon Hill. No one was there
for jay-walking. Dimming, kitchen lights signaled
an electrocution powered by International Harvester's
generator. There was the smell—factories or flesh?
Newcomers clothes-pinned their noses. From her two
story brick town house on Main Street, Ellen Glasgow
was sure the odor sweated out of Appalachians crammed

into *penitentiary bottom*. No society novelist like Glasgow
who won 1942's Pulitzer Prize for *In This Our Life*,
your mother, ever the optimist, insisted living next door
to the pen was a good thing; escapees would put miles
between themselves and cells they'd left. Shirts and pants
missing from a neighbor's line, you knew boys who made
it out were not cold. Breaking away naked from a shower,
skin blended into night more readily than zebra stripes.

No convict, you needed more than clothes to escape.
If you failed in school, you would commune with other
bruised things. Slowly like a dog, turning to tamp a bed,
you created order: cards, a William Faulkner bibliography
used to write your books. Day and night, shuffle of work,
your mother never found steps to a dance. No circus artist
balancing without a net, she did drop you a rope to swing
away from a life that was a long shutting down of her heart.

ANNE YEATS

My father, I board the bus to find you
in another of your trances—humming,
beating iambic pentameter with your fingers
curled on knees. My mother had warned me
over and over I dared not deprive the world
of your genius, to never interrupt. Lines
of a poem you were composing in your head
might be another *Sailing to Byzantium*. Silent
in the house, I was careful where I stepped
like a squirrel on a utility wire. Believing
I had proved my virtue day by day like
a daughter of the Confederacy who leaves
daily roses for the dead at Appomattox,
I hope you will move over and make room
for me on your bus seat, in your heart,
say *Anne* as if I am a star. No. An iron filing
around a magnetic source, I get off behind
you at our gate. You turn, seeing a strange
ten year old girl at your side, ask, *Oh, who is it
you wish to see?* I am unable to answer, *my father.*

You Had the Choice, Martha

as you clocked second month: gut, firm
flat dinner plate or inflated rubber glove.
Despite the doctor's warning, you did not
have your son sucked out, preserved in saline
to let the technicians sample fetal bone.
Like a suitcase, you lugged your stomach,
elastic as Siamese skin upholstering two bodies.

Blasphemy of love you cannot now abort:
Lesch-Nyan. One in one hundred million,
but when it's yours, a statistic isn't a number
but a child. Your heart burns at words that bother
him so, whispered from that irreplaceable face.
You do not love Robby less for his caged heart
or because he must always be lifted to the van,
hands tied so he will not gouge out his eyes,
teeth pulled to stop gnawing at arms. Scars
are the letters you must keep him from learning,
knowing he is taught nothing by the pain,
but that it feeds a need that can never be filled.

Spoon him your dreams, even though your son,
the trickster, spits them back on the kitchen tile.
Slip, slide, skate through. Lift your arms, an angel
in flight in spite of what you do that is so human:
buying the blue bicycle, propping it by the bed in
Robby's room, building a ramp that you know he
will never pump, coast, or brake, flinging gravel.

WITH MY GRANDFATHER TODD
THE SUMMER I TURNED SIXTEEN

Take jewelweed, you told me, for the sting
of nettle, digitalis for a broken heart. The bells
of jimson weed were bitter but pennyroyal
with small lavender flowers spread over

a field was the sweetest of wild mints. Heal
sprains with comfrey, rashes with goldenseal,
burns with aloe. To show me passion, you
compared foxfire, a luminescent fungi even

in decaying wood and leaves, to fifty years
of love for Grandma. Picking blackberries,
you wore brown leather fish gutter's gloves
that my father brought you from Maine.

Because the fingertips were cut out, you could
feel the fruit, soft like a heart, ease it off briars.
The juice, the lard crust of a hot cobbler were
worth pain. No way you knew to keep them

from being born, you took me to the creek
with you to drown kittens where they'd wash
away, making me watch, telling me not to give
life to anything I couldn't feed. Your lesson held

on like moss through the years when I needed it.
You are not here to celebrate tonight, the ninth
of July, to guide your great-grandson, Todd.
As he turns sixteen, I'll give him a circle of gold

you hammered from a coin for me. Your ring
will remind him as it did me that sometimes
it's not just the bad we do, but the good that can
turn on us as a surprise when we need it most.

Sooner Was a Hard Dog to Keep Under a Porch

Strapped to a body you can only remember,
in albums, you are still my father. To keep up

strength, you slide your walker from the kitchen
to living room as if skating laps in suede slippers

color of honey. You're sure moving hands, feet
will deliver you just as your mother's hand

saved Sooner. Scraping a chair across the kitchen
to sit next to me when I peel potatoes, you show me

your bones are stronger, you can lift your left leg
without putting your hand under it. A calendar,

your years ripping off day by day, you follow me
wanting to talk. I fold towels, roll socks. You're there.

Still your daughter, I listen, but your stories never
tell me what I want to know, what the photographs

cannot say about my grandfather, my grandmother.
The story of Sooner was different. The short fingers

on Grandma's hand attracted me, not their picture,
your account of the wedding night, the *shivaree*:

Twenty men kept them awake by carrying a blade
from the saw mill on two poles, took turns clanging

with ax handles. Their years silk scroll through you,
stop when Sooner's picture unrolls the stand of corn

Grandpa bought in Oklahoma. It shriveled. The poodle
meant enough to haul him back in the covered wagon

to Kentucky. Sooner could fight, got dogs twice his size
in corners, knew to go for the feet. Then, it's a sheep

killing on the farm by roaming dogs. Used as Grandpa
was to slaughtering hogs, it was not a pretty sight. Ones

maimed had to be shot. A week of cleaning, picking out
blood, wool clotting branches did not remove the stench.

Grandpa warned his neighbor, found his collie running
loose by Rough Creek and shot it. He could not, would

not abide the sight of any dog on his farm. Ears open,
eyes shut, you understood a boy's place in a man's world,

could say nothing to save the dog that held your heart.
My grandfather's voice was soft, never out of tune.

When he called to Sooner, it was no different than
the hundreds of times they'd gone to chase a rabbit.

Sooner knew, hid under my grandmother's skirt.
Grandma stopped sewing, put her hand on his head

right where she knew the bullet would go. It was
not her left hand, finger banded in gold. Twisting

in her chair, she used her right, the one that peeled
potatoes, kneaded dough for biscuits, the one that

Grandpa would shatter along with Sooner's skull.
Their eyes may have met, a vein of defiance might

have throbbed in her neck, but no words were needed.
Mindful there was always enough food to go around

a second time, my grandfather, knowing the order
of things, the fiefdom, the serfdom, hung up his gun.

WHITE CHICKENS

The image of a straitjacket has come back to me.
Flat, folded together, sleeves open and reach out
like white wings flapping the backyard my father
fenced trying to be Grandpa who reined in chickens
that ran, nested in the barns, and laid eggs in hay.
Never a one-sided chase, did the cackle, the flutter,
the attempt to flee cast iron pan whet his appetite?
Telling me he learned colors from the blue-tinged
gizzard, green gall bladder, red blossoming in water
used to bucket away blood, Daddy didn't answer when
I asked if he loved the nub of heart, lungs that held
no more breath than a small purse, suck and release
of the esophagus being pulled down through the neck.

Because our chickens were bred for slaughter, they
were packed in crates after hatching, raised standing.
Daddy's new batch of fryers were too weak to walk.
The optimist, each morning before his coffee, he
lifted them from the chicken house he had built,
positioned them, statues on the grass of three roosters
and thirty hens that had been cooped up too long.
It should have been easy for him to wring their necks.
Pecking at corn, they would have given up without
a struggle, refusing to scatter. Was it boyhood need
for thrill of the chase that left him unable to kill or did
my father expect our chickens to rush the yard, twist
off their own heads and plaster grass with their blood?

PITCHING OUT EIGHTY-SIX YEARS

Driving my father to Erlanger from Lexington
to clear his Kentucky childhood out of Uncle Paul's
house, it is not the talk about his brother's death
but his own that keeps my foot on the pedal, one
car length ahead of a semi overtaking us on I-75.

Jiffy labels stuffed into black plastic, rubber bands
around Kroger bread wrappers for control, dragging
bags to the curb, it's empty bottle after blasted bottle
of Mrs. Butterworth's syrup I curse. Each morning,
Uncle Paul forked waffles from the toaster. Beans

one day, potatoes the next, he'd stop smack dab
in the middle of Dixie Highway, pick up a Coke bottle.
Fingering his brother Paul's wedding picture, my father
reminds me of Dorothea Lange's photographs, teaches
me what five cents meant to a man who lived through

the Depression. Sit a spell just for the company,
Daddy says while he reads shoebox after shoebox
of sympathy cards, allowing as how none of his words
will be printed by Hallmark, just his name chiseled
on stone. To distract him, I lift up shoes from Maude,

Snip and Nellie, work horses with feet big as dinner
plates. Bingo! Out we go. As long as his knees hold out,
my father coaxes me into watching him throw ringer
after ringer as his mind dandelions to cropping outside
Cecelia. Sixty years ago, for him, anything was possible.

Wound into sleep by his feet, his poodle, Sooner, sealed
out August heat. Stepping stones down the hillsides,
my father and his brothers framed earth in split rail
or creek rock, as if even earth needed to know its limits.
Justus and Paul right up alongside him, growing six acres

of burley on the halves, their only cash was tobacco
sighing in the back forty. Before my father had sweated
off Snip, Nellie and Maude's winter fat, he had to toe
a wooden box to reach across their shoulders, flanks, then
crawl under belly after belly to fasten snaps and buckles.

Disk harrows, turning new ground, they had a three-horse
hitch, only one in Hardin County. Paul on a foot-guided
sulky cultivator, Justus rode the water tank of a setter.
Between working tobacco, my father and his brothers
mowed on machines with pitman rods rattling like bones,

cutting bars chattering as if it were December. Briars
and fescue fell, as orderly, as precise, as the first soldiers
to hit the beach on D-Day. One hundred and seventy-five
acres to mow, Nellie set the pace, let my father know
she was finished by nuzzling his shoulder. Marking off

the land, circling until everything was leveled, my father
took his time, sitting pretty like he does right now with me
in Uncle Paul's basement. A Kentucky Derby banner
felted in 1936, two rulers from Abe Lincoln's birthplace,
cedar boxes from the Smokies and a set of walnut skittles

carved at Boone Tavern are like cutting down weeds.
My father can see where he has been. How long can I
stay still, sit watching him unwind a story from every
ribbon Uncle Paul ironed? How can I keep him from
looking ahead at the few rounds left for him to mow?

How a Daughter Justifies Poems about Her Father's Cancer

My father's a lucky man,
not like those ducks
on Grandpa Todd's pond.
A boat of white feathers, feet
were the first to be gripped
in jaws that had stayed beneath
layers of silt, eluding fish hooks,
husbanding survival. Only a thin
life line of bubbles to surface
betrayed the turtle. A burst
of muck air, no picture
or headlined obituary recorded
a death so quiet, a death so small.

First Blood

My grief's raw, hangs hooked like gauze-shrouded ham
curing in the smokehouse, or mitoxantrone and aredia
that drip into my father's right arm. His left hand

nooses my wrist. Chained by my love, by the bracelets,
the necklaces, he had made for me from field clover tied
head to stem, I can't repeat bone scan, last PSA count.

To distract my father, to pass the three hours, I read
the sports page, quote the latest in the battle for the title
of home run king. Taking off a Cincinnati Reds' hat,

fingering his long white hair to impress women tubed
up in other hot pink lounge chairs, my father can't resist
spouting statistics. It's Those Yankees he remembers:

The Team in 1927. That summer he was barely thirteen,
doing the work of a man, hauling logs, baling hay,
driving his daddy's Model T. In their regular season,

taking 110 games, Those Yankees swept Pittsburgh
clear out of the World Series. One-handed, my father
can still wow the ladies showing how he swung a broom,

cleaning the Pirates right out of the stands. Yankees'
percentage of .722 in regular and post-season games
was the best ever. Babe Ruth hit 60 homers, more than

every other American League team. Just twenty-four,
Lou Gehrig hit 47 runs, accounted for 175 RBIs—what
fans like my father called *ribbies*. Just warming up, he

gets started on Hall of Fame pitcher Herb Pennock who
won 19 games. That's it for me! No roots in Connecticut,
my mind's back in Cecelia, Kentucky, the cellar house

where Grandma kept green mason jars she filled last fall.
Needing peaches, lard to fix a pie, she called me *sissycat,*
tried to shame me into going down alone; after supper,

my father came along. No light, boards were rotting on
the stairs, so we were quick, mapping out fruit ordered
in red, yellow, white, gold. If the cellar door clanged,

I knew his hand would hold a flare of wooden matches
he used to light kindling each morning for the coal stove.
Spiders tied nets; my father went first to break the veil.

HERRING GULLS ARE DECISIVE

Holding out for McDonald's french fries, refusing
week-old hamburger buns, apple cores I scatter
above frozen foam that waterfalls sand, these birds
are like my father who leaves ham, red eye gravy,

even cornbread I fix to make him forget the nausea,
two more months of chemotherapy, a Yankee winter
he's settled into. At low tide, ice shaped like lilypads
holds seaweed in place; for us each day's more unstable

than Morgan Point's shoreline. A crossover to beach
is frozen rock and hard going in the harbor wind
from New Haven that sweeps this inlet. I'm seeking
metaphor in a kite tail tangled in evergreen branches

by our seawall. I settle for goldenrod, injecting winter
stems with memory of September, of yellow flower
feathers clustered with monarch butterflies and bees,
strung like lights out of season on a Christmas spruce.

Scrub pine that takes what comes, my father refuses
to give Lexington post office a new address, to put
one root down in Connecticut. Unwilling to give up
going back home to Kentucky, he tells me goldenrod

is his state flower. Like him, one isn't just like another.
He lists categories I can use as a fieldguide: plumelike
and graceful; elm-branched; clublike and showy; wandlike
and slender; flat-topped. I clip stem ends, brown as sable,

for him to examine. Rigid oval upper leaves clasping
hairy stems, my father is positive it is hard-leaved
goldenrod found west of the Appalachians. Nothing
I say gives my father such certainty, nothing I cook

brings him comfort. He thinks only about surviving,
longs for hollows not shore. Filled with emotion, I am
useless, have no way to release my father, guide him
with eyes that are frozen like stone in sockets of sand.

Moonflower

Silence wakes me more surely than a scream.
At three in the morning, sound on a baby monitor
is what I listen for: my father clearing his throat,

motor of hospital bed, flushing of toilet. It is
to him, to his movement that I am bound. Mouth
yawning, arms stretching like petals, he wakes

and then sits on the bed's edge to avoid vertigo.
Sallow skin, the cream yellow of moonflowers
whose stems tighten around their few minutes

of glory, of life, my father curls fingers on a cane
handle abandoning his pride. Driving, my lips
twisted into a handkerchief at a funeral, his death

is what I can't escape. At the dentist for a crown,
sure enough, my chair faces tombstones I count
while black plastic bags acrobat the cemetery walk.

Afternoons, asleep in his blue chair, my father is
so still, I stand until I am sure tissue paper whispers
of lung rise and fall in an eggshell chest. When will

I shawl it in tattered rosebud from Howe Valley?
By spring, will I be a supplicant by a dogwood next
to his grave, hands palming air as white petals do?

Bound to movement, there can be no escape from
the cross of this earth for my father until the stigmata
on dogwood petals pinwheel over him in the ground.

Rigor Mortis

Trying to suck in life that was being withheld,
my father's mouth opened to death. A nurse
might have smoothed his eyelids, but no one

pinched his cheeks together. Someone cared
about his hands, crossed like corpses I had bent
over in Civil War photographs at Gettysburg.

On the shady side of the railroad tracks, lined
up like silverware at a buffet, those not blown
apart had their boyhood restored to all my father

had been, green as Kentucky fields he plowed
in Howe Valley. Once, but not now. Daddy
outlived his body. Could death have been

a surprise to him? *Oh, this life does end. No more
potatoes and onions fried in lard, or windfall apples
to peel.* By the time I found my father laid out

for me to view in the chapel of Hospice, I could
not slice the O of his lips and force them together
as I do with parentheses on my laptop's screen.

No medical degree, I did not know, did not want
to ask a doctor how many hours it takes for a body
to harden, how long it will take for my heart.

THE SWAN

I know bad children who charm swans
with bread crusts, then strike them

on their necks with sticks or with stones.
I would like to compare myself to a woman

who halted I-95 traffic for an hour to let
a pair with four cygnets cross, but here I am,

not paying attention to where I am casting.
Snagging a swan in the wing, I cut the line.

Not deliberate, an accident, but the result
is the same. There is no way to remove

the barbed lure that will stay like careless
words, hurt I've done that I did not mean

to do. Rattling on, I told my mother I would
not marry a man like my father who preferred

the company of sharpshooters, of danger
to mine. How could I know my mother had

lodged my boast in his heart? Praying for grace
that would make me quiet, blessed, I listened

to my father the night before he died. Daddy
had not closed his heart, but spoke of what we

trade, what we keep, what we must let go of
now that we would be in separate lands of earth

and air. Returning my words that had nagged
him for over thirty-five years, my father gave

me the chance to clean his wound so his death
would not scrape, be a burl, a gnarl, a bone

in my throat, like that hook in the swan's wing
I could not extract or wrap in cotton to shroud

trail of monofilament glistening in morning sun.

Assigned Reading: Betty Friedan's
The Feminine Mystique

To provoke, *Child, you don't have sense God gave a goose,*
I pound a stake smack dab in the middle of my side yard

for a bird feeder I brought with my mother from Kentucky.
I realize a sharp-shinned hawk will attack songbirds while

they eat unless I shelter the tube under the kitchen overhang
like she did. Never opening windows in order to keep out dust,

her life has been spent indoors. No wonder she doesn't know
a male hawk's back is gray, or a female's is brown with fawn

barring the breast. It's a waste of time and money to order
Darwin's *Origin of the Species* for her, or point out how birds,

all of them, can be fed by this new link I have just created
in the food chain. I'll grill marinated chicken breasts tonight,

even though I know my mother won't eat them. I want
to hear *back when I was a girl on the farm,* how many necks

she watched my Grandpa Todd wring, and how a rooster
could circle longer without its head than a hen. Like Formica

counters she windexed three times every day, her mind
has been wiped clean of what it can not bear: the cleaver,

the pounce, talons of the hawk. Sunflower seeds that I poured
in the feeder have lured two sharpies who will cull my garden

of those who fail to keep watch, those too restless to hold
a pose, who don't heed a thin high scream, two feet of wing.

Frozen in forsythia, a titmouse touches its bill to a twig
and two chickadees tilt heads skyward to escape predators,

as I have had to do, first by speed, now by sense and stealth.
I know how a greater pain drives out a lesser one, and what

can pierce then empty all I have caught in the cage of my ribs.
Skewering me on a spit, memory will dart like a hawk, soar,

dive, then pull up, circling back in a flight I cannot tether.
Earth is what it is, what it needs to be. What am I to do

if I get up each morning, but accept this world, be like
my mother, learn to empty my heart of what it cannot hold.

02-14-99

This snow is what I pray death will be.
I am released from myself, from guilt for
not driving across Whitney Lakes to visit
my mother in The Arbors. I can excuse
myself as easily as I do from a table. Moved
with my father, his cancer, from Kentucky
to Connecticut, my mother gave her past,
her present, her future to me. If I don't visit

her here in this Yankee state, no one will.
Instead of memories, the lima bean I lodged
in my ear, she keeps a list: emery board, Q-tips.
My mother does not search for a way out, press
the code, 02-14-99, to open locks as I did each
day, every day when I lugged her to my home
to visit my father imprisoned by his ribs, black
lines on a bone scan. Their fifty-eight year

marriage has been forgotten as if it were a hotel
she checked out of in July. My mother's path
circles corridors: nursing station, hairdresser,
back again. Lost, her feet keep shuffling,
keeping pace with her walker, patent purse
tightened over her shoulder. I admire packets
of Kleenex she won at Bingo the night before,
how she threads marbles of glass. Unstrung

by the recreation therapist each evening,
each morning is a resurrection for my mother.
Wearing her gift of beads I finger into a rosary
of worries, I wonder if like my golden retriever,
my mother can make a decision, get up from
a rug, walk, think *bed*. If I would extend my palm,
offer her our communion of beaten biscuit and
country ham, could she remember the taste?

Dreaming of Spring Break while Installing a Bird Feeder for My Mother in The Arbor's Courtyard

No Bharatpur Bird Sanctuary in India, or Pantanal
in Brazil for me, I would head for Papua, New Guinea,
the Tari Valley. No novice, I can reel off 43 species,
20 genera of birds of paradise. Eight were spotted

last year at Ambua Lodge where I could palm time,
not close it into a fist. I'd keep notes in present tense:
true plume birds, flagbirds, riflebirds, perching birds,
birds of paradise ranging in size from thrush to magpie.

The largest and best known bird is *Paradisaea apoda*
whose cinnamon-yellow head and neck, emerald throat,
reached Europe on Magellan's ships. No such luck
for a gray squirrel in Connecticut eyeing kernels I pour

into three funnels. Like Satan in Milton's *Paradise Lost*,
this Yankee squirrel contemplates *His sad exclusion from
the doors of bliss*. Even without wings, his paws will find
a way to our sunflower seed. *Just like a man,* my mother

says. I'm startled by her voice, as if I didn't know she
was right next to me. I tell her males spread plumes in
courtship, and to begin breeding, hang upside down on
trees, sit on twigs as if waiting to step on a dance floor.

Diphyllodes magnificus flaunts a yellow, erectile cape,
two long wires coil from the tail. *Lophorina superba*
raises a black velvet cape over its head. My mother
whispers she never saw my father naked during the day.

No need to tell her males don't participate in nest life.
A faithful daughter, I can give my mother what's on earth,
a heaven for birds I can mount on a pole. If not *Paradisaea*,
then feathers of cardinals, wrens, robins, pigeons, crows.

Morning Glory

It's pink punctuating boxwood with exclamation points
that hooks my eye. Shell pink, lady pink, my mother's nails,

cascade over the fence to the street covering foil wrappers,
cigarette butts, bottle caps. A girl who'd read anything,

I even memorized names of morning glories in *Burpee's:*
Carnaby Red, Brazilian Orange. My girl cousins named me

Weirdo because I liked tie-dyed blossoms of Flying Saucers,
ordered the macabre, the midnight black of Kniola Bowles.

Prissy Sissies, they wanted Blue Dawn, Scarlett O'Hara,
Pearly Gates, Robe, and Wedding Bells with three inch

lilac blooms that could camouflage the outhouse we stuck
back in the hollow. Morning glories thrived on neglect,

didn't bloom well in fertile soil, required no deadheading
and preferred to forge upward with no interference from me.

I spent my summers keeping them from stealing sunshine,
sapping soil, water, from strangling the field corn. I'd uproot

twists and tangles, but it was as impossible for me to kill
that heart-leafed vine as it is for me to clear out dementia

which films my mother's mind. Her dress misbuttoned,
a flash of humor glows in the center of her face, a lamp

through fog. She tells me she never let on she knew I hid
in ditches, watching for flashlights, for the game that went

on in the night, for older boys that never came for me.
I can wait for her to resurface again, but that could be days

from now. Peering as my mother did while hanging quilts,
I cannot find some loose stitch that I can mend any more

than I can cream years from her face with Pond's. She cries
when I leave. My love for her like morning glory, impossible

to uproot as it vined beans, okra, tobacco, has found the way
to collapse my heart. Pushing, finding my limits, like a beer

can I bend in half with my thumbs, my voice cracks under all
I want to say, and cannot because I hold a small girl's hand.

ORPHAN

Not a word one would apply to a sixty-two year old,
but it is the first one I think of this Thanksgiving,
the first since my mother's death on Memorial Day.
On the table, I position paper turkey napkin rings

made in her Alzheimer's craft group six years ago.
My father was too weak to sit; Mother as if playing
at being some other wife, insisted I place the one
lettered *Charlie* on his tray. In two months I wouldn't

need to make her visit him, letting her rest in the car's
back seat before loading her walker into the trunk.
Each napkin ring is different, as if colored by a child
in Pre-K. Never a jaywalker, Mother no longer cared

if red, orange, or green on her turkeys stayed in lines
that had controlled her life and mine—*Iron your blouse.*
Wear a slip. Land sakes, girl, are you going out looking
like that? Marrying to escape my good daughter self,

I left Kentucky, Methodist church revivals, pledges
not to drink alcohol and called Connecticut home.
Today, I am free of all that. Yet, why am I bothered
by the erratic mess my mother made with her box

of Crayolas? Like her, I worry knots of what I can
not undo, words like *stupid bitch* I used to hurt her,
the college graduation she would not attend because
I wore only a slip under my commencement robe.

With no way to show her that I pick up my clothes,
don't leave pizza crusts around my house, writing
this poem is like tapping a code on a cement wall
not knowing if the cell on the other side is empty.

Praise for My Son's Photographs
of Harlan County

Leaning on the Yale fence, your hands are my father's hands
    fingering ribs of his horse. One day it did not rain,
then another. A month, then another. The earth wrinkled as

if it had pores. Grandma opened the Bible to *Deuteronomy:*
    The earth over your head shall be bronze and
the earth under you iron. Easy choices were already made;

grass was gone, hay, corn too pricey. Cows, auctioned off
    before their time, were a dead loss. Harder choices were
to come, not like the decision of a judge who had no trouble

awarding first prize to photographs you entered in Saybrook
    College's graduation exhibition. Your grandfather
stands at the edge, his face half turned to center as if trying

to pull away from something, someone beyond the frame.
    Daddy's rolling a cigarette in paper too delicate to pencil.
There is coffee I cannot smell. Even in black and white,

you didn't reduce life that couldn't get much bleaker to gray,
    drain the color from furrowed cheeks no longer held
up by teeth. Cropping the ragged edge off truth, you might

have airbrushed liver spots on hands. Pulling your head out
    from the cover of your box frame camera, you positioned
my mother, stood her next to my father, rocking on the porch

of Mack Quiggins' store. Texaco kerosene on the right, gasoline
    on the left. Metal signs are still nailed to outside walls:
Chesterfields Satisfy; Sweet Scotch Snuff; Old Gold; POP Kola

and *I'd Walk a Mile for a Camel.* Times when a piece of ham
   in the house would have scared us children to death,
Daddy was still proud he could farm, not work for wages.

Nights after supper, after praising her biscuits, her pole beans,
   he'd remind Mama how it was a hard get-by between
Rough and Meeting Creek, how he'd have to grow a cash crop

so she could shop at Uncle Louis Paul's in Arch. Times change.
   An archaeology major, you tell me how you will grow
sunflowers, live in harmony with the earth, how some caches

of seeds dating from 3000 B.C. have been found in Tennessee.
   How could you know about chopping with a hoe, peas
frozen in the field, selling tires from the Ford to pay for food?

No one had the chance to snap a picture of your grandfather
   walking out of Kentucky, resting with suitcase in hand
beneath a billboard of a man lounging back in a chair under

a caption: *Next time take the train, Relax.* Daddy got all the way
   to Texas. The Panhandle. It was a hard country. People
wouldn't help bury you. If you died, you were dead. That's all.

III

ICE BITES INWARD

White has been dropping
as long as you can remember.
Running through March snow
you feel it fall behind you.
At a certain moment, the ground
is no longer brown the way
day drifts to dark. You almost
see color go, but you always look
away just as light is evaporating
like the last drop of water
on asphalt. When you exhale,
there is a cloud. Will a thought
slip in, cause you to miss
the breath that separates a moment
from your last? Flakes fill the night
one by one, countless like years.
In such whiteness, ice invents itself;
never look up or back, only on.

AND THEY, SINCE THEY WERE NOT THE ONE DEAD, TURNED TO THEIR AFFAIRS

—Robert Frost

Shirtsleeves rolled or starched collar turned up
to Kentucky wind, it's always men who share
coffin weight up Science Hill to where it's flat

enough to dig a grave. The oldest women kinfolk
will have done their job, moving a black rectangle
from border to center of a burying quilt covering

the lid. Sitting with my mother in The Arbors,
I unfold square after square of Celia Farmer's
heirloom of darkness our family has passed down

like a pocket watch. On the blue flowered edge,
four coffins remain. I knew I was breaking tradition
by unraveling thread before my mother's death,

but sewing was a tourniquet for my nerves, one
way I had to wear down the clock. Suspicious
by nature, living in tomorrow, done with today,

Mother wanted to be sure her quilt was ready, told
me to line her casket up like a used car by graves
of Burnadean and Hazel, her sisters who had gone

to their reward. When I put down my needle, there
were three scraps to move. I named mine *obsidian*.
Wallowing like Grandpa Todd's gray hog, I wonder

if two sisters living in distant states that I can only
travel to when grief or marriage unites us on a pew
will move my coffin to center. I have already paid

for eight Connecticut gravesites so my three sons
won't have to climb up Science Hill to level ground.
The family plot I own is above the Branford River.

Tide was out, muck exposed when I chose the land.
Worrying about a view I wouldn't see, spotting ospreys
nesting on a platform above the green marsh, I wanted

my feet pointing to their perch, not subsidized housing
on the hill. Controlling what I can, I am comforted
by knowing what spot of earth is mine. Will I learn

to accept tide as the river does? It's not incoming water
high in cattails, but the going that undertows, leaving
mud slicked on sticks like bones of an opossum I can't

resist eyeing on morning walks with my retriever. As
its body dissolves, skin blackens to shine like wet earth.
No quilt for the opossum. It's easy to accept a death

that is not Mother's, not mine. What I fear in others is
myself—that I won't pause to mark the morning I don't
pull my dog away from the opossum, from what remains.

Merryfield

—for David Engstrom

I should preface this by saying I do not rescue ants,
sail them out the back door in a paper towel. Standing
by a stainless steel table waiting to end my dog's life
was the first time I witnessed a death other than ones

I'd caused on a kitchen counter. The mercy was the end
was swift and looked easy. I already had a metaphor:
a poppy's catarrhal rasp spewing death rattle of seeds.
A rose would have pricked Taffy's shaved leg harder

than our vet did. If there was terror, there was no sound,
nerve jumping, nothing. In spite of the face I'd watched
turn white, beauty of red hair over ribs, I dismissed offer
of pet cemetery or ashes to scatter, reasoning the body's

a body, not soul or lantern. Bones corseting her liver,
a tumor was the only flesh growing. Taffy would walk
to her dish, look, only to turn away as if the word *water*
was forgotten, but not the thirst. Cubes of beef filet

stayed untouched by her paw. The glory of flesh was
that it operated even though Taffy would not eat or drink.
Shrinking, my dog did not turn into something else.
A golden retriever, she dug holes where she could retch.

On her last morning, taking advantage of an open door,
as if digging her grave, Taffy burrowed under junipers
as I searched to leash her for death. Did she understand
it was not my world, but hers that would not continue?

ON THE ANNIVERSARY
OF MY MOTHER'S DEATH

My phone call to my youngest sister a mistake,
What's up, her hello, then silence with a syntax
of its own. With no bookends, first it was our father,

five years later our mother. I can see my mother's
body in hers; but blood we share can't knit childhood
wounds: wrists broken falling onto the gym stage

after I pushed her, my knee split on creek stone
when she tripped me, the scar above her lip I bit
that still turns white in the sun. Airfare too high,

we don't visit or phone, just e-mail monthly pictures
of grandchildren, and order gifts on-line at Christmas
and birthdays. Using my book of poems as a coaster

to protect a cherry table, her fingers wrapped around
a Starbucks coffee cup are stuck like fish bones
caught in my throat. To stop myself from sending

angry texts, I go to lunch—fried shrimp, my solution.
Before ordering, I watch as owners, the six Chello
sisters, bone Connecticut River shad. It beats going

to the ballet. According to Micmac legend, originally
the shad was an unhappy porcupine who asked Manitou,
the Great Spirit, for another form. Turned inside out

and dubbed shad, the porcupine was hurled into
a river. An ichthyologist counted the bones: 769.
Sitting elbow to elbow, thigh to thigh as if playing

chess, the sisters roe, scale, behead, split. Boning
100 pounds in 12 minutes, they compete—a record
is three slashes, 37 seconds to slip a sheet of filet

off the cutting table. Sisters, laughing at shared jokes,
one with candy red polish, her middle nail stripped,
reminds me of my sister, her pedicures, and manicures,

who is repulsed by my frayed cuticles, cracked heels.
It is as if my sister's heart and mine have taken
different turns in a childhood labyrinth I can't escape.

What created years of dead end paths: possessions,
privacy, pecking order, parental love? Seven years
younger, my sister and I never shared a room, grabbed

the last ironed blouse. I never had her as a personal
servant to carry my lunch box to school. Did we ever
walk Dixie Highway to the Gayety Theater in Elsmere,

her coat sleeve against mine? Maybe in spite of our age
difference, we were no different than the blue-footed
booby pushing brothers and sisters out of the nest to die,

or embryonic sand sharks that eat each other in the womb.
The sister I'd like to find is the girl on my mantle framed
in silver; under a sign *Pikes Peak or Bust*, she is laughing

and pointing to the split in my pedal pushers. Splashing
each other in Simone Hotel's pool in Miami Beach,
we could have peeled skin off each other's backs. She

might have let me bury her in sand. My co-conspirator,
she would have smuggled a flashlight so I could read
Nancy Drew past bedtime. Even if I could wring out

a past, my hands can't twist us like a rag into girls again.
A porcupine with no god to transform me back into shad,
my bristles were turned outward for armor, my tongue

the sword: the call, driving alone in the middle of night
to view my father in Hospice next to the shopping bag
of clothes; the stone I bought for our parents, the one

my sister never praised or visited. The years piled on
years of her silence have maimed me. So many hurts,
if my sister would say *Sorry,* I would not know why.

I don't know what it is she needs to forgive: me telling
her at six years old to get lost, walk back to our cousin
Marilyn's house in Milwaukee. Kleenex for breasts,

I was thirteen, wanted to parade down Lake Michigan
hoping boys would form a line under arborvitae bent
in winter. Crying, my sister wandered street after street.

If I were a mathematician, I might say the depth
of my need for her love increases in direct proportion
to my power to estrange us. Like a B. F. Skinner rat,

rewarded one time in a thousand, I never quit, hardwired
for the luckless lottery, loved the god of my cage who
on my birthday would surely call, send cake crumbs

tumbling down. Memory like pinfeathers of down
from Grandma Todd's geese pricked my neck at night
when I punched or wrestled my pillow. Another dream

of another childhood, I believed my sister and I could
start again, straighten all lines that were crooked, avoid
dead ends. I knew my sister wouldn't sweeten my days

as they pancaked, but hoping all love had not been
sucked like marrow from our childhood, I invited myself,
flew to see her. On the plane, perhaps memory's warning

to my heart to stay on the surface or because I did not
have a fried shrimp lunch to distract me, I remember
eating shad I bought from the Chello sisters. On top, fish

was mushy but the deeper my fork rappelled, the more
intense the color and taste, and the texture became
firmer, hardening like years I couldn't unpleat. No one

to meet me at the airport; stepping from a cab, I learned
my sister would be at a wedding she forgot to mention
and wouldn't be home for the weekend I'm there. Once,

anger like tulle igniting would have flashed, now even that
had fizzled, my smile sagging like a slow leak from a tire.
When I set off her alarm and police came to see if I was

an intruder, if I could have found the picture of my family
I had sent, it would have been a rush I could not name.
So many chances to connect missed, and missing again.

TUMOR

You're the middle sister—no Bach's Mass in B-minor
for you, but Jimmy Buffet with his hush puppies on
over and over in your head. Temporal lobe seizures,
a tumor has jimmied its way into your brain. Knitting
at what you can picture, say, a cat, the word escapes

you. After the MRI when death hovered, wings like
a black butterfly, doctors gave you no time. Hoping
for a change in diagnosis, to downgrade *astrocytoma*
Stage 3 to Stage 2, I try to put positive spin on a biopsy.
To distract you, I spout about trepanation from Greek

trypanon. Over 8,000 years old, boring into the skull
is the first known surgical procedure. Perhaps religious
rite, initiation into the priestly caste or for demonic
possession, a hole in the head served as mouthpiece
to the gods or a window that would give bad spirits

an escape hatch. I ask if doctors have read Hippocrates
and Galen's instructions about the operation. It may
or may not be a good idea for my sister and me to watch
the film *Heartbeat in the Brain,* the December, 1970
production by Amanda Feilding, a twenty-seven year old

art student who treated her head as if it were a piece
of sculpture topped by a floral shower cap. Filming
herself, she pumped a foot pedal to dental drill a hole
into her frontal bone. Dropping like ripe plums from
their seats, front row members of the audience fainted.

Changing a tunic blood-spotted in carnation-sized
stains for a Moroccan kaftan, Amanda bandaged then
wrapped her hair in a shimmering gold turban. Saying
goodbye to the camera, *Drilling a hole in one's head is*
really a nerve battle, she headed to a fancy dress party.

Mary Alice, you have also made an art of holding
yourself together. After radiation, chemo, I bet you'll
use the hat covering your scalp to play Frisbee—snatch,
cartwheel toss, shouldering through. Covering pillows
with cockatoos and hibiscus, you are a woman who

uses star fruit in salads, are thoughtful just like the man
who dropped a glove on the train platform and threw
the other one from the window so someone would have
a pair. I believed I was hardened, would chip at Lot's wife
to salt my steak, but today *glioblastoma*, the Stage 4 tumor

that fingers your right lobe, strangles my morning. At night,
on my back, I look up at the star cluster called Beehive,
its other name is Cancer, the crab. Brave, I picture you
without a bee-keeper's veil, canvas hat or leather gloves
among the swarm, hands open to the sting. The oldest,

my job was to wash your hair in the kitchen sink. Perching
you on a stool, neck like a swan, I lathered warm water,
got suds in your eyes, down your back, your shoulders
sharp as sparrow wings. When will your hair begin to clog
the shower drain leaving nothing for my hands to hold?

This Is Bluegrass Country

Two that don't love can't live together without them.
But two that do can't live together with them.
    —Robert Frost

Farmers who own the fields on either side of us
where thoroughbreds graze could not agree
on common boundaries. So, there's a story I can
tell you about the path we walk. With no interest
in economy or being good neighbors, each has
built a white wooden fence leaving a passage called
Devil's Lane. This land has never been an Iroquois
battleground so we won't even bother poking
around for arrowheads. Standing between pastures
freshly mown, the grass green as our uncoached
kisses, my arms are bare to a heat that predicts
lightning. If it should strike, you remind me, don't
cower under a tree; go stand in the open. Leaning
on a fence post, you compare our love to gauge
blocks, machine shop measures that don't need
anything except trueness to keep them together.
That day, there were no shapes for the words we
walled in, would not speak, or the anger we hung
up to dry and then mounted like cardboard pieces
of an African puzzle you glued on a mat to frame.

SURVIVORS HAVE VICTIMS

We turn in time from what will destroy us, if we can,
gathering what of the past we can hold: my grandmother's
plate of full blown yellow roses scalloped in gold. Coming
to take what was left of my mother's cherry chest after
the tornado outside Somerset, Kentucky, all we found

were drawers on a foundation strewn as if by a thief ignited
by absence of money or jewels. We walked Pulaski County's
red clay roads that summer my grandfather's farm was
leveled, looking for a dish, a photo. The twister sucked out
cows as the barn flew apart, boards lifting like souls going

to heaven in Raphael's *Transfiguration*. You said our love was
like Natural Bridge we crossed the day after our wedding,
predicting we would leapfrog old laws that forbid marriage
of Gentile and Jew. You were the wandering jew, a plant
named not for a willing immigrant but an exile impossible

to control by pinching vining tendrils with purple undersides.
Clover, there was clover everywhere we stepped. With
no tattoo of blue roses like my sister or black numbers you
could recite from your father's forearm, I tied stem to flower
to double wreath my wrist. Picturing gloves made from

baby skin you saw in an Israeli museum, you transformed
Buchenwald and Belsen into a grand rounds: to experiment
with labor, a woman's feet were not raised like a mare's in
a blacksmith's shop, but thighs strapped together. No exit,
life was peeled from its core. Like paper dolls I clipped out

and strung together, words could never metaphor mothers,
their wombs sealed into a mausoleum. When I saw you were
holding your breath in the shower, I knew you were testing
how long you could go without breathing if water stopped.
No common boundary for miles separating us, Germany

to South Africa to Kentucky, of course I felt your ethical rage.
To meet challenge of years I couldn't pull myself through,
I could only mouth despair, the Holocaust. In time, there were
fences between us rising like hot air or the gas I couldn't breathe.
Knowing what cannot be swallowed must be spit out or it will

rot like strings of meat caught between teeth, I choked on earth
Nazis planted with your family's ashes. I could not block their
shadows, could not pull three sons away in time from the flames
our anger created. If they smoldered, you fanned them to keep
fire burning, burning through years that can never be consumed.

Romeo and Juliet, Act V, Scene iii

—William Shakespeare

Chopsticks straightened, sucking orange sections, I pour tea
and recall driving around Kentucky. Concrete bridged a road,

black paint dripping: *God lie to us.* Blessing's cookies do. I snap
dough to unthread your fortune: *Things are difficult before they*

are easy. The printed strip won't circle you like cancer rubber
banding your father's stomach. Snagged by a hook he cannot

remove, trying to die, he can't let go of breath that's squeezed
flat. Stretching for your son, clots of snow hung as he drove off,

leaving the fish tank half filled with neon tetras, metal speaker
from an old battle ship but no note. Divorce shovels my life;

three sons will learn where their father is by watching him run a
marathon on TV. A coach, I bark orders: *You can't swim a river*

without getting wet. Sucking on red wine, dissecting two movies
we had rented at Best Videos to analyze impact of directing,

you puzzle over constancy of Romeo and Juliet rather than
debating whether Laurence Harvey's dramatic display of passion

in the balcony scene erased the final act in the tomb. I try to start
an argument over merits of casting: Castellani's use of known

stars versus Zeffirelli's unknown youths. Instead, you feast on
Juliet's last moment of steel: a love that stays will get us through.

No Six Pounders

One legged weed in shallows, a white heron
passes the time, aim of its bill more accurate than
my son's hook. Each night after Eric was born,

I was an ear, fearful his breathing would stop,
but sleep has come back into my summer like dark
does, always catching me by surprise. Yanking out

sprays of sea grass, I clear sand to let our beach
rush to new growth like I had done. A cormorant
dives, making a wake in slate faced water. A scar

healing, the surface closes over what swims beneath
as I try to distract my son, keep him from repeating
the question I pretend I do not hear. I can explain

that the cormorant has webbed toes, a hooked beak
and an appetite for snappers that can't be filled.
As I describe how fishermen in China double knot

a silken rope around one leg, using the leashed bird
to catch fish, Eric interrupts to ask why his father
doesn't call, visit or bring his boat to take him fishing.

Satisfied with my answers, distracted by the bobber,
his bait is swallowed by huge striped bass we imagine,
but never catch. At Master Bait and Tackle, pictures

of men holding blues are our lures. Mounted jaws
of sharks caught off Morgan Point keep us casting
and casting. My son is sure that if his father were here,

we would catch fish after fish; he waves to every boat
going by just in case it might be him after all. To pass
time, we use a coffee can to trap a crab, then another.

Again, there are questions about why his father hunts,
but won't fish and others I can't answer. No scientist,
I don't know why lobsters turn red when boiled, but I

know there is a difference in deaths. Our fishing hook
is not like the bullet his father used to kill a fox so he
could snip its tail for the Harley he has bought to ride.

Unnatural

Once the Valedictorian, now the father, you flinched
as the son you acquired by marrying his mother flapped
the graduation stage, gown open, diamond stud earrings
and sunglasses glinting. You were grateful his last name,
not the same as yours, melted into another. The question
had become not class rank but of getting a degree. Four
years taken from you could not be regathered like apples
from a basket he smashed. Moving *Grateful Dead* posters
like leftovers from a tag sale, you gave him the chance
to reinvent himself. Your sentences scraped nothing,
not even membranes of his sleep. A pillow sandbagging
his head, was he laughing at you during a daily morning
ritual: lies you told the principal; notes you wrote for
the body that would not get out of bed; patches you
plastered on holes his fist put in doors? Did fighting ease
his anger, or was it that younger brothers were outside
listening to him numb you with *fuck this, fuck that?*

Guns and Roses, Pink Floyd or *AC/DC* blasted through
on CD's you had paid for, on speakers too large, too heavy
to be hung from chains anchored to the ceiling. *Nirvana*
gave him the words: *chokin' on the ashes; all we know, is all
we are.* Reminding you that it wasn't just sticks and stones
but words that could hurt you, he would hurl, *Jagger's old,
just like you, Dude. Both of you should've packed it in before
you hit thirty, showed some real class and pulled a Cobain.*

Guilt had grown stale like water standing for days in a glass.
Too much about injustice, divorce. Too much bailing water
from a ship, holes left by the father, the natural father, he
would never please. What could you say about the man?
Step was salt Eric rubbed on your skin each day. After he
spit in your face, you learned how unnatural this son, love,
could be. No smile or thumbs up in your camera's direction

as he waved the diploma aloft, the only sign he gave to you
was a turning of his face, the way a leaf must to the sun.
Grafted, the new life you had given him had not taken.

After the ceremony, you went to The Chowder Pot
to celebrate but your son punched rocks into the water
as if he was trying to fill Long Island Sound with stone.
If the two of you had been on either end of a boat
separated by mist and not by different blood, this son,
this unnatural son, knew he would have no need to call
out your name but could sit waiting for the slushing
of your oars. No sextant, nothing was left for you but
to hold steady, rowing blind in a fog that might never lift.

FUNGUS-YUM

I am twenty, not fifty in this dream
and when I get to The Boston Garden
to see the Grateful Dead, there is a boy

man who has set up shop selling hookahs
outside the concert. I walk up to him
to ask what they are and he turns.

It is my son, at least my son's face,
pasted on a long tangled mess of curls.
He tells me I'm pretty, I remind him

of someone but he can't figure it out.
I pretend I know just what to do,
that the hookah is a waterpipe used

to smoke marijuana, grass, stuff, paper,
what I called Mary Jane. He tells me
he's at Yale and I want to understand

why he has set up shop outside the Garden
selling hookahs. It's the good paper he
had riding the T, what a blast it is to light up

in front of other passengers; it's how
he usually checks out people selling before
a rock concert, but now people check him

out as he checks them out; how perspective
is completely different; like it's how he
totally loves it. I ask if he needs money.

He describes his mother, her phony ideas
of success. I use his language: *wasted, suck,
dude, fucking A*. I ask how much the pipes

are worth, where he got $500 to buy them,
what he will do with them during the show.
To show his faith in society, he'll stash

the hookahs in a hole where a stairway
has broken off.   He'll put a bag there, go
to the Dead's psychedelic concert with me.

It's not going to be as total, as awesome
as the old Renaissance Fair Grounds,
their best show in 1972, but it'll hang.

When *Candyman* comes on, it's Vince.
The boy man with face, body, hair
of my son gets pissed at Jerry during

Broken Arrow; Phil is having the best time
and Jerry is staring at his shoes. Why
can't Jerry look up and see Phil having

the time of his life? *Space* is long and kicks
ass. I reach up to caress the boy man's
face, my son's face because in this dream

I am twenty and I am not his mother, I
am a Dead Head. Still, I do not understand
him; I cannot wake up from this dream.

REPETITION AND VARIATION:
BIRTHDAY POEMS FOR MY SIXTIES

At the end of his life, Beethoven devoted
days, weeks working thirty-three variations
of an insignificant waltz written by Diabelli,
a composer of no great distinction. Turning
sixty, I know why. Straining for music to seep
into fingers, his head, Beethoven leaned on piano
keys as I do on memory, my son's childhood.
Sending him to YMCA Camp Beckett, I believed
he'd learn to pitch a tent for shelter, use a compass
so he'd never erase the way home, but thirty years
later, he is still teetering at the rim of the lake
diving for the first time, trying to suck air.

I.
No Emeril, cooking never interested me—even
a jam cake to mark my sixty-first birthday, but I
used to compare my son to yeast in dough.
Edging over the rim of a bowl, pushed down
he would rise again, become all I hoped he could
be. I knew he'd never be a Beethoven, but I would
have settled for being minor like chamber music
of Borodin. Today, it's not bread but my mother
I remember. Angry—I'd ducked Sunday school
or sassed her in front of the preacher—she would
pump her Singer sewing machine as if it were
bellows of life support she could tube into me.

II.
On guard like the lookout in a bank robbery,
watching for my son to lurch into the parking lot
of Eli Whitney's bar near Sleeping Giant Park,
I remember a story I told him about the evil giant

Hobbomock who stamped his foot in anger
and caused Connecticut River to change course.
Why can't I find a good spirit like Keitan, swift
as wind and a spell caster, who netted Hobbomock
in darkness, turning him into a six mile ridge?
What I like best about the myth is the triumph
of good over evil. What an ecological message—
the Blue Hills, columns of basaltic trap rock
running east-west with haze blanketing the profile
of a body, sleeping or passed out. A footpath parts
brush that opens to a cliff overlooking New Haven
and Long Island Sound. If it were 1735 when
Joel Munson built a grist and saw mill near
the giant's head, my son would have found a horse
or knee-walked through corn fields like Uncle Paul
did. But, even in a time of whale oil, hollow wick
lamps and tallow, I wouldn't have been able to snuff
candles on my cake, let darkness swallow my son.

III.

I repeat a birthday promise to quit living
with dread, salved only by daily checking
my back yard for what I do not want to find—
my son slumped over staining the teak bench.
No matter, one way or the other, there is no
ransom for years I should be celebrating. I have
only one past sutured by four letter words: *love,
pain, hate*. If I were a high wire star who could
drop a trapeze for her son to catch, we might have
many futures. Would any of them be duty free?

IV.

This day matters to me but not to a check-out girl
when I can't stop myself from telling her it is
my birthday. I know what I'm missing—a sense
of the absurd. Year after year, it's the same: write
a poem about my son, his past that nothing can
appease, even veins sluiced with lithium. Footprints

were always in front of him: a father, the doctor
who mourned for himself not his son's shuffle from
job to job. Absent so long, he calcified into a man
my son did not recognize walking right by him
in the hospital the day his brother had heart surgery.
He was startled like I am by an unexpected mirror:
a blotched fossil with red vining my cheeks, mouth
turned down as if I'm gritting my teeth. Was my father
giving me advice about aging or about love, its grace,
when he showed me how to press my lips to the side
of pears that struck the dirt? *There*, he'd say. *There*.
Anyone with a ladder could pick perfection. No flaws,
stemmed to top branches, green fruit was not as soft,
not as sweet. Like my son, ground pears bruised from
the fall were grateful to be chosen, to be touched at all.

V.

Not quite resting on the guillotine of old age,
but unable to muscle my carry-on into a plane's
overhead bin, I should watch the moon sliver,
court dawn when rain has injected root smell in air,
not gravedig into sleep to forget my son's roaming
soul, flailing, stilled only by a drunken stupor.
No stars rhinestone Morgan Point. Muffled
in cloud, a lighthouse on New Haven's breakwater
foghorns, but can't help me search for him,
my oldest child, now almost forty. Bar to bar, I
hope to palm keys, take the Volvo I'd given him
for safety. Sure I see his car, like a firefly, then I
don't, then I do. I picture a mason jar my father
used for moonshine, how I took a sip when
he turned to pet Queenie. Throat coated in fire,
my eyes teared like they did today when I
opened the gift my son had crammed in the
mailbox for me: *The Bipolar Disorder Survival Guide.*

VI.

I abrade myself with couplets, enjambments,
anapests, iambs but if a loofah could scrape

my son from me, I'd have a birthday massage.
Kneaded and reamed as if I were a lemon,
perhaps I'd pay extra for a foam. Like a ball
of yarn I refused to bend and pick up when
it was thrown to me in a circle of his rehab
group during a therapy game, my life
unwinds, crisscrosses but there is no
pattern, no way to untangle, take control.
Once I thought he was a gift to my womb;
now, I buy dented cans of black beans
as a reminder of how to love. If entering
another year could be like turning
a doorknob to find another son, would I?

VII.

Elbowing out of his burgundy Mercury,
vintage but not preserved, the man selling
The New Haven Register at the bottom of
the State Street ramp could be my son. I have
a red light; he does not get up. His car door
is open. Smoking, he leans on his thighs.
Orange vest, his arms are a macramé
of faded burns, cuts, welts, not from barbed
fences or baling hay, but his overalls sag
with dirt that could've come from suckering
tobacco in Kentucky fields. This man
might be my uncle, my cousin. I cannot
stop staring at his thick brown head of hair,
his furrowed cheeks that arrow my heart
back into Appalachian hollows. If his mother
drove by him as I do on my birthday, would
she be grateful he is not dead, buy a paper?
I picture him walking Hamden's Skiff Street
probing seams for change in couches, chairs
left on the curb. I wish I had the clear bags
of cans and soda bottles I rinse to leave by
Shop Rite for people who need the five cents,
redeeming what they can. This man is not
my son. My light is green; I can drive away.

VIII.

My left knee is artificial. There is a limit
to what I can replace but I am trying *ostranenie*,
making strange, to see my son as if he is
brand new: cub scout leader, church deacon,
soccer coach. I don't search his car for vodka
or lock the liquor closet. Like the loon, my cries
have haunted each summer, a tremolo at night,
alternating notes to mimic an echo; my poems
have been a call going out and then returning—
a prayer without a response. Dare I believe
my son has taken the impact of his steps, and
weight of his two sons into his own hands? It is
possible my words for him have been the bell
of a fishing boat sounding out what had not
yet drowned, have clotted into a raft carrying
him from shore where he has found new ground.

IX.

The Russian critic, Viktor Shkovsky, taught me
The man who has lived all his life by the sea does not hear
the sounds of the waves. It's low tide. A birthday gift,
smell of piled shells washed in Morgan Point's cove,
does not drive me back into the house. If thoughts
about my 69th birthday could be like rotting snails,
cleansed by being emptied of life, I might make
my mind uncouple its heart, not just *recognize*
but *see* my son, accept that he has changed. What
would Beethoven have said of his life, of his final
obsession with Diabelli? Each variation composed
in one key, he transposed it to another but always
with a refrain that was repeated, as if trapped like
a plant hopper, wings spread, trying to fly first from
resin, then entombed in amber. Encased in a past
he attempted to escape thirty-three times, was
Beethoven ever able to create a new context?

Fireflies Punctuate the Night

Our hands parentheses in the back field,
I know I am tempting my little sisters with
Don't look, don't look to be sure. Just one peek
and gold inches out of their reach, a lure

blinking like a Captain Marvel watch. In July,
in blackness, we nail five holes in metal lids
of our mason jars. I never figure out where
fireflies we don't catch go at dawn—under

porches, magnolia leaves, maybe Uncle Lanny's
Farmall tractor? I don't forget morning's lesson;
my sisters choose to not remember. Botanists
observing okra seeds left overnight in glasses

of water, they see ebony swelling to opals. I
find fireflies gulping like Harlan County miners
tunneling for air. Bugs, they teach me nothing
about loss or searching earth for what has no

answer like Demeter did after her daughter was
pulled from her through a pore in the ground. I'm
no goddess in mourning negotiating with Zeus to
send Hermes as messenger to his brother, Hades,

demand he return Persephone to surface. Palming
fireflies, thumbs pressed together, I can cup light
until wings tease open my hands, but not my heart,
allowing life to be carried into darkness, into night.

Connecticut State University Distinguished Professor, Vivian Shipley teaches at Southern Connecticut State University where she was named Faculty Scholar in 2000, 2005 and 2008. Her ninth book, *All of Your Messages Have Been Erased* (*Louisiana Literature* Press, Southeastern Louisiana University, 2010) was nominated for the Pulitzer Prize, won the Sheila Motton Book Prize from the New England Poetry Club, the Paterson Award for Sustained Literary Achievement and the CT Press Club Award for Best Creative Writing. Her sixth chapbook is *Greatest Hits: 1974-2010* (Pudding House Press, Youngstown, Ohio, 2010). She has received the Library of Congress's Connecticut Lifetime Achievement Award for Service to the Literary Community and the Connecticut Book Award for Poetry. In 2015, she won the Hackney Literary Award for poetry. Other poetry awards for individual poems include the Lucille Medwick Prize from the Poetry Society of America, the Robert Frost Foundation Poetry Prize, the Ann Stanford Poetry Prize from the University of Southern California, the Marble Faun Poetry Prize from the William Faulkner Society, the Daniel Varoujan Prize from the New England Poetry Club and the Hart Crane Prize from Kent State. Raised in Kentucky, a member of the University of Kentucky Hall of Distinguished Alumni, the highest award the university can bestow on an alumni, she has a PhD from Vanderbilt University and lives in North Haven, Connecticut with her husband, Ed Harris.

Praise for Vivian Shipley

In our society, distinctive locales are being leveled. Drive across the country on an interstate, the distinction in landscape disappears into Burger Kings, Domino's and Walmarts. Vivian Shipley's poetry preserves a uniqueness of place.
—*The New York Times*

Vivian Shipley explores regions of the quotidian terror: erasure, the double-death of ceasing to exist and ceasing to be remembered. Being loved, or at least understood, serves as one remedy against erasure. She exposes the lie in easy dismissiveness and demands that we be better than we are. Poetry exists for a higher purpose than delivering information or asking questions. Shipley reminds us implicitly that poetry, unlike terror, survives, giving voice to the eternal.
—*War, Literature & the Arts*

To take on voices or compose dramatic monologues is nothing new, of course, but what is remarkable is Shipley's facility at imbuing voices with the same conversational, even casual tone as in her autobiographical work. The readers feel as though we have sat down together with a cup of coffee or maybe a stiff drink, and a life is being shared.
—*Prairie Schooner*

Poet of both heart and conscience, Shipley spans centuries as well as continents. Again and again, Shipley becomes the voice of innocents condemned to death and of their guilty condemners who go free in poems that are complex, dense, primarily narrative, but often with breathtakingly lyrical moments.
—*The Texas Review*

The language Shipley uses is extraordinary. At times, a line may leap off the page and become a banner the minds-eye sees and can't quite move past. Often, her description is painfully stark, ridged, as if it were happening in the present. The reader can't help but take it personally, the sudden desire to remove yourself from your chair of comfort and demand justice.
—*Rattle*

Shipley's sympathy is genuine; she succeeds in transplanting her voice into other vessels across history, showing a common humanness and need. —*New Letters*

There are no small deaths for this poet. First person narratives pre-empt death's shuttering silence by preserving her story and those of loved ones. Poems center on her parents rooted in terminal illnesses: the father's prostate cancer, the mother's Alzheimer's, the daughter's need to wrestle past and present. —*Caduceus: The Poets at Yale University's Artplace*

Shipley shows us the various walls we are locked behind—jails, senses, things, memories. If Shipley doesn't always show the reader a possible way out, she at least makes our prisons more visible to us through the beautiful enclosures of these well-made poems. —*Hampden-Sydney Poetry Review*

Shipley focuses on those who might otherwise disappear in the shadows. She brings them vividly to life, with all their complexities and whether or not we would be so inclined otherwise, makes us care about them, for they are so very human. —*The Hollins Critic*

The voices in this collection rise above Shipley herself as if she were channeling the dead: we recognize her artistry in this book, but it feels like we are having a conversation with lost souls. —*The Briar Cliff Review*

Made in the USA
Middletown, DE
27 July 2015